# A Manual of Foxhunting

# A Manual of Foxhunting

Captain Ronnie Wallace

edited by Michael Clayton

SWAN·HILL

PRESS

## PHOTO CREDITS

The author and publisher are grateful to the following for permission to reproduce copyright photographs in this book: Douglas Lees page 133; Jim Meads pages 19, 30, 33, 38, 39, 41, 67, 73, 80, 85, 88, 91, 93, 97, 101, 107, 129, 132, 135; Stuart Newsham pages 28, 51; Peter Pritchard page 77; Tunbridge Wells Advertiser Co Ltd page 7; Wellington Journal and Shropshire News page 114.

Every effort has been made to contact copyright owners but in a few instances this has not been possible.

First published in the UK in 2003
by Swan Hill Press, an imprint of Quiller Publishing Ltd

**British Library Cataloguing-in-Publication Data**
  A catalogue record for this book
  is available from the British Library

ISBN 1 904057 128

Typeset by Phoenix Typesetting, Burley-in-Wharfedale, West Yorkshire
Printed in England by MPG Books, Bodmin, Cornwall.

# Swan Hill Press

an imprint of Quiller Publishing Ltd.
Wykey House, Wykey, Shrewsbury, SY4 1JA, England
Tel: 01939 261616 Fax: 01939 261606
E-mail: info@quillerbooks.com
Website:www.swanhillbooks.com

# CONTENTS

Appendices

# INTRODUCTION

In 1966 I asked Captain Ronnie Wallace if he would grant me an interview for a book on foxhunting I was writing. Partly I suspect, because I was at the time a staff TV and radio reporter for the BBC, Ronnie was exceptionally helpful. He was well aware that foxhunting needed as many allies as possible in the national media to help combat the growing battle for the future of the sport against the animal rights fanatics who wished to ban it. Finding a news and current affairs broadcaster who was besotted with foxhunting was unusual and potentially useful.

I took a tape recorder to Ronnie's home, which was then at Glympton Park in the Heythrop country. As soon as our interview began I was impressed by his lucid, consistent answers. It was clear that Ronnie brought gifts of clarity and organizational ability to his sport which were exceptional.

At Glympton I met the remarkably beautiful Rosie Lycett-Green whom he had married two years earlier. She was to prove during many years of warm hospitality I enjoyed in the Wallace homes in Gloucestershire and Exmoor, to be one of the kindest people I had ever met, especially when times were bad.

I enjoyed their company enormously, and I began a staunch friendship with Ronnie and Rosie unconnected with my own value as a journalist, continuing until his tragic death in a road accident thirty-six years later, on 7 February, 2002. At the age of eighty-two he retained his exceptionally sharp mind; he had a close interest in politics and an astute appreciation of the bigger picture; and still had much to contribute to the best interests of the sport which was his abiding passion.

Ronnie had a talent for long lasting friendship, and there was remarkable testimony to this in the acute sense of bereavement of so many who mourned his passing. His funeral on Exmoor, and the remarkable memorial service at Stow-on-the-Wold were attended by people from an extraordinarily wide range of backgrounds from all over Britain and abroad.

During my twenty-five year editorship of *Horse & Hound* we

often worked together closely to protect the best interests of foxhunting not least in the area of public relations. He was an excellent listener, and would seek advice on many subjects from a wide circle of trusted friends and allies, although he kept such advice in separate compartments, and then made his own decision.

There was one extraordinary aspect of his personality of which I was sometimes uncomfortably aware: he was hypnotic in his ability to gain control of other people's time and practical support. Curiously, it was almost an extension of his talent to direct his hounds.

Yet, in the same way that he gave hounds freedom as well as control, he made a clear distinction in his human contacts between those he could always control, and those he could hope to influence without expecting slavish obedience.

At *Horse & Hound* I maintained a practical working relationship, as well as our friendship, but at the same time took care to emphasize my independence. Ronnie handled this with sensitivity: I do not recall an open disagreement, let alone a dispute, on any of the subjects where we happened to disagree. He simply walked around such areas, and concentrated on matters where we were in agreement. For example he was opposed to changes in traditional Hunt dress, whilst I was an early proponent of all horse riders using modern safety headgear, including chinstraps, because I was so aware of the inordinate number of deaths and serious injuries in a sadly changed Britain where people were more likely to fall on hard surfaces.

I was one of those who felt that Ronnie was somewhat too slow in his latter years as Chairman in stiffening the MFHA's self-regulatory procedures, and rules clarification. He addressed these matters in due course, and supported further acceleration of much needed change by his successors in the 1990s.

There were just a few individuals at local and national levels with whom he had head-on clashes and where friendships were permanently fractured, but these were remarkably rare in the long life of an individual determined to dictate the course of events. My friendship with Ronnie and Rosie remained intact because they were such caring and amusing companions.

Above all, I cherish the many years in which I rode after Ronnie in the hunting field, marvelling at his genius in handling hounds in the enclosures of the Cotswolds and the wilder spaces of Exmoor.

His occasional fierceness with his staff and followers in the hunting field was doffed immediately the day was over, and how I enjoyed his informal company after hunting. He cloaked it with an increasing air of gravity, but he possessed an enormous sense of humour.

My defection to the joys of riding to hounds in Leicestershire and Rutland, where I was to make my home, evoked only keen interest and support from Ronnie. He had his reservations about some of the 'riding people', but he well understood the traditions and values of Shires hunting, and its importance in the world he sought to rule.

Despite his own knowledge and authority, he much enjoyed hearing and discussing others' experience and views on the sport.

For this reason I am particularly grateful to Ronnie's great friends, Marty and Daphne Wood, Joint Masters of their own Live Oak pack in Florida, for permission to reprint Ronnie's remarkable panel discussion for the US MFHA with the great American Master and huntsman Ben Hardaway. It gives a flavour of the mind-set of two of the greatest foxhunters of all time, widely different sometimes in methods, but agreeing on the fundamentals of their sport.

On the practice and achievement of best standards, Ronnie was unassailable. Many of his friends regretted that he had never put pen to paper in producing his own handbook of foxhunting. In the year before his death he asked for my help in assembling and editing articles which he had contributed to the sporting press, usually in interviews which he carefully checked before publication under his name. Other friends and disciples agreed that such a book would be of significant value to a field sport which still commands widespread support in Britain, Ireland, France and some other areas of Europe, widely throughout North America, and in most Commonwealth countries.

## Acknowledgements

The major threat posed to the future of British foxhunting by the Labour Government's Hunting Bill introduced in 2002–3 has made the publication of this book even more important, and I am indebted to Swan Hill Press for undertaking publication of this work, following their publication of the excellent biography, *Ronnie Wallace – the Authorised Version* by Robin Rhoderick-Jones, in 1992.

We are especially grateful to Julie Spencer, Editor of *Hunting*

*Magazine*, and the proprietors, St Martin's Magazine plc, for permission to reproduce verbatim interviews on hunting by REW which form the major part of this book (in Chapters 2, 3, 4, 6, 7, 8, 9, 10 and 11),and similar thanks are due to the management of *Horse & Hound* for reproduction of interviews with Ronnie Wallace (in Chapters 2, 9 and 12) which appeared in my book *Foxhunting Companion* (Country Life Books, 1978). *Conversation with the Master* in Chapter 1 appeared in my book *A Hunting We Will Go* (Pelham Books, 1967). Thanks are due to Hugh Robards for a brief quotation from his book *Foxhunting in England, Ireland and North America* (The Derrydale Press, 2000), and similarly to Daphne Moore, from her book *Famous Foxhunters* (Spur Publications, 1978). My appreciation is due to David Wallace, son of Ronnie and Rosie, for his help and encouragement, and to Rosie for making available photographs from Ronnie's own collection, and access to some of the obituaries he penned for others. I am grateful to the distinguished former MFH and hound breeder Martin Scott for reading the manuscript. Many will share special gratitude to Stephen Lambert, a notable successor as Master and huntsman of the Heythrop, for permission to reproduce in this book his tribute to Ronnie at the memorial service, held at Stow-on-the-Wold on 19 March, 2002.

Michael Clayton
Morcott, Rutland
2003

# MEMORIES, MEMORIES . . .

Ronnie Wallace's death was marked by a memorial service at St Edward's Church, Stow-on-the-Wold, on 19 March, 2002. This was the heart of the Heythrop country where Ronnie had forged his great reputation as a Master and huntsman. The Church is only a few miles from Eyford Knoll, the home where Ronnie and Rosie entertained so many hunting people during the twenty-five years of his remarkable Mastership.

The church at Stow was packed, and many more friends and admirers attended in overflow accommodation in a tent and a hall with loudspeaker relays of the church service.

There was unanimous approval for a fine address given by Stephen Lambert, formerly one of the young Masters and huntsmen who were so much influenced and instructed by Ronnie. Stephen, son of the late Uvedale Lambert, a Surrey landowner and Joint Master of the Old Surrey and Burstow pack, had served with distinction as a Master and huntsman with the Taunton Vale, the Warwickshire, and finally he was a successor of Ronnie Wallace at the Heythrop.

His address charts Ronnie's life and achievements with affection and humour as well as insight.

'*Would you just see to that?*' How many of us here this afternoon have heard those words addressed to us by the Captain? Generations of us; earthstoppers, hunt staff, colleagues in the MFHA, politicians, hunt supporters, Masters of Hounds, terrier men . . .

One of Ronnie's most trusted and long standing colleagues in the MFHA said last week, 'I've spent most of my working life *just seeing to it*'! Ronnie's instructions were never that easy, but, surely, the *command* to see to this service and speak about his life must be the ultimate in delegation.

It is impossible to stand in Church today and do him justice in mere words. Captain Wallace was and always will be a legend: a man without any equal in the world of twentieth century foxhunting, and by any measure, one of the most remarkable personalities among Englishmen living in the past half century.

His life and his influence were founded on an enormous wealth of gifts and talents. These included a very sharp brain, incisive judgment, an encyclopedic knowledge of people and how they ticked, how they were connected with each other; an intimate knowledge of the heartbeat of rural life, and above all, a talent for organization that underpinned everything that he did.

He was a detailed planner, a born teacher, a delegator supreme, and with an intense determination to achieve the very highest standards in all matters connected with foxhunting. His presence was absolutely compelling. He touched the lives of innumerable Masters and amateur huntsmen and generations of hunt servants in Britain, across the Irish sea, and even in the United States.

Countless numbers of hounds bred by him went on to become famous on the flags but, much more importantly, performed brilliantly in the field. And yet, alongside his single minded dedication to foxhunting, he had immense interest in many other areas of life, of which politics was perhaps the foremost.

## The pinnacle

Without doubt, he reached the pinnacle of his career at the Heythrop. He was thirty-three when he arrived in this country in 1952 but in the previous sixteen years or so, he had taken every conceivable opportunity to hunt hounds, and to see other top class huntsmen in action. This meant that he was enormously experienced, not just at hunting hounds when he came to Chipping Norton but also at running a country, ensuring that it was crossable, and that it was well foxed.

He already knew an immense amount about hounds and their qualities by then, partly because he took immense trouble to listen to the pundits, amateur and professional, but also because his time with the Hawkstone, Ludlow, Teme Valley and Cotswold, had given him plenty of opportunity to try things out. Unlike most of us, he learnt quickly by what went wrong.

Looking back, it is easy to see why the great things he did, he did so brilliantly. The early period of his life laid many foundations for what was to come.

## The Eton experience

His first official pack was the Eton Beagles and he broke the record in both of his two seasons as Master and huntsman. In 1937–38 he caught seventy-five brace of hares and three foxes. His first fox was the one caught at the opening meet of the Beagles in 1936. It was accounted for in the copper tub of a cottager at Eton Wick. The leading hounds had checked. All appeared to be lost until the shouts of a lady were heard: 'Hey Mister! There's a great big rabbit come into my kitchen, broken the lamp and jumped into my copper.'

Asked by Ronnie's whipper-in Colin MacAndrew, later famous as Master of the Zetland, whether she was sure it was a

His hunting background: R.E.W.'s father, Eden Wallace (right) at the opening meet of the Eridge in 1926, with Lord Richard Nevill, in tweeds, Lady Camden and Lord Henry Nevill.

rabbit, she said: 'Yes! It's a big brown thing with a long bushy tail!' Mercifully, we are spared further details!

The Christchurch Beagles followed while Ronnie was an undergraduate at Oxford University. Next came a spell in East Anglia with his own beagles when he was a serving soldier in the war. As the foundation of what was to come, his time with the Hawkstone Otterhounds was of critical importance.

## The Otterhunting years

With typical Wallace planning and forethought, Ronnie's father had taken the Hawkstone 1938, so that REW could hunt them. He did so for some thirty years. He considered that otterhunting had more venery about it than any other form of hunting. Skill was needed to drag up to the otter and find it; other skills were required of both the huntsman and the hounds at various other stages of the hunt, whether on water, or as often happened, on land.

Out with the Hawkstone he was able to try out other types of hound in the field in a way which could not be conveniently done foxhunting. This was where he first tried out Cotley bred hounds

Capt. Ronnie Wallace at a meet of the Hawkstone Otterhounds of which he was Master and huntsman from 1946–68.

(West Country Harrier blood), and where he first started working with Welsh cross hounds and Dumfriesshire blood.

One other important contribution of the otterhunting years was the vast knowledge it gave Ronnie about so many different parts of England and Wales. Whether whipping in to Ray Thompson at the Wye Valley, as he did before the war, or visiting with the Hawkstone, he hunted from Devon to Norfolk, Wales, and many other places, including Ireland. This gave him an accurate knowledge of how hunting worked in different parts of the country and the sort of problems that Hunts faced. Such information was intensified when he started the Puppy Show rounds as a judge that were to become a major feature of his life. Thus, when he became Chairman of the Masters of Foxhounds Association in 1970 all sorts of Masters looked to Ronnie for advice because they knew that he understood their local difficulties.

From the otterhunting years there emerged many well known names and friendships which remained for life. They included John Robson, who is here today, and of course, Anthony Hart, who hunted hounds when Ronnie was not available. By 1968 Ronnie felt that he had to hand over the Hawkstone Mastership. It was not unknown for him still to be otterhunting when cubhunting was at its height in October and the national hunting scene was taking up more of his time. Most importantly, otters were becoming scarcer due to river pollution, and the ecological viability of the sport was in question.

[Later Ronnie Wallace led a voluntary cessation of otterhunting in the United Kingdom because of the decline in otter populations, providing a remarkable example of sporting conservation. The decision took great tact and diplomacy, but it earned the practice of registered hunting with hounds much respect. Wallace was able to illustrate that the enemy of the otter and indeed other wildlife, was not hunting but the loss or degradation of habitats in the countryside. Otters were being rendered infertile through chemical sheep dips and industrial waste in Britain's rivers.]

## Charles Parker and the start of a system of earthstopping and fencing

What name is synonymous with Ronnie's years at the Hawkstone, Ludlow, Teme Valley, Cotswold and Heythrop?

Charles Parker, of course. Contrary to popular belief, Charles hunted hardly at all with Ronnie at Eton. His family home was and still is in East Anglia, and it was in the war years that he first helped Ronnie when he hunted the Trinity Foot country and the Swaffham area.

Furthermore, Charles hunted on horseback, sometimes with a terrier on his back, when Ronnie had the Ludlow, and he continued to ride in the Teme Valley season and for the first year at the Cotswold, helping much more in kennels and in the stables than with terrier and spade.

At the start of their second season at the Cotswold a decision was made that Charles would not ride, but would concentrate on stopping and field work with the terriers. Much effort went into covert laying and producing fox friendly places. At the same time, Ronnie organized a system of hunt jump construction, largely organized by a great enthusiast, Alan Martyr, from Ablington.

## Arrival at the Heythrop

After four years of top class sport at the Cotswold, and with Raymond Barrow from Farmington now Field Master, and with Richard and Charm Fleming from Leygore having a foot in both camps, it was inevitable that there would be a push for Ronnie to come to the Heythrop. Not everyone agreed. Superb sport at the Cotswold led to outrageous accusations of cheating, and Ronnie's home life was not perhaps at its most reliable or tranquil. He got home as a new Master by a majority of one vote only at the Heythrop annual general meeting. In 1952 Ronnie began his twenty-five Golden Years.

## The Heythrop

What was the secret? It was compounded of many elements: the best Hunt Staff; Charles Parker and many others who helped in the country, and after Charles, Desmond and Roger; the best Foxhounds; the best Huntsman. There was wonderful backing from his Chairmen and Hunt Secretaries; and the Heythrop had, and still has, some of the best and most sporting of farmers and puppy walkers in the whole of Britain; plus the most generous and enthusiastic of land and estate owners, most of whom hunted.

Chief of these were the Flemings, the Kleinworts, the Schusters and the Wills. And then there were marvellous places such as Adlestrop Hill and Sarsgrove, which acted as fox reservoirs. On top of this was Ronnie's unlimited stamina; and his unstoppable appetite for organization. He hunted every inch of his own country, and I may say, a fair chunk of his neighbours' too! In Warwickshire, earths mysteriously became stopped when the Heythrop were meeting near the border.

Other major plusses were some of the most attractive topography in the world, which attracted rich people, almost all of whom Ronnie vetted so as to be sure that farms and estates went into the right hands; a bevy of helpers of whom the chief were Stella Towler, who looked after the horses, Lavinia Jenkinson, who ran the fencing and farmer liaison for so many years; and Diana Hastings; and a succession of hugely supportive and generous Joint Masters, such as Pam MacKinnon, who was with Ronnie for twelve seasons; the late Lord Dulverton for seven seasons; Ted Marsh for six seasons; and Lord Rotherwick. These people supplied very considerable financial backing and enabled the Heythrop to be run at the highest possible standard.

These factors came together to make the Heythrop what it was throughout those twenty-five years. But it was the Captain who orchestrated it in the most brilliant, idiosyncratic and charismatic way. Whoever you were you could not take your eyes off him, especially at the meet.

When he arrived, the hounds would make a huge noise as a welcome; enough to shift any wise fox in the vicinity I should have thought. Even watching him climb on to his horse was a magisterial performance. Then came a procession of countrymen to give him information; the briefing of the hunt staff and field master and those famous scouts, several of whom are present here, who used to go forward and see a good fox.

This was one of Ronnie's chief characteristics, whether on or off a horse. He always wanted information, which he would file away with a grunt. Where he filed it in his mind was closely linked to his opinion of the reliability of the informant!

The departure from the meet was often late, but immediate action regularly took place, especially when he wanted people to spread out as quickly as possible. A fairly constant stream of rollickings flowed, which were unique and ultimately killingly

11

funny because the expletives were so astonishing: it was not unusual to be addressed as a f*****g poached egg if one had failed to spot the fox at the critical moment!

He never forgot a face; he loved visitors, he took enormous trouble with them when they came to hunt; he adored the young, and he was very, very kind to the old. He and Rosie were also the most generous hosts at home, and also hugely welcoming in the hunting field, (though Rosie went like a lamplighter out hunting and most visitors were hard pressed to keep her in sight!) Ronnie himself always took the easiest route on a horse as he wanted to keep himself in one piece and hunting hounds, but if there was no alternative, he would jump a house, especially on Bertha.

He was, for obvious reasons, unhappy about shoots taking place in the Heythrop. He was equally reserved about the training of racehorses too, for reasons that are less clear! A certain senior NH trainer, not unused to giving rollickings himself, found fault with the conduct of the Heythrop on his gallops and lectured the Captain. To his astonishment he was informed, 'if you want to train f*****g racehorses, beggar off to Newmarket!'

In the 1970s a video was in circulation entitled *Hunting and The Farmer*. It featured Ronnie and the Heythrop. Serious in nature and certainly showing hunting run by the Captain in the most professional light, it was nonetheless amusing.

A dark, wet night. Headlights approach. A very wet and muddy Captain Wallace emerges from the car. Tap on the door. Door opens. The loose handshake.

'Do come in, Captain Wallace.'

'Ah Mr Fellows, we have had the most marvellous hunt from your covert. Seven mile point, actually, and caught the fox at Taynton. I'm very pleased to say that before hounds went away, they caught that barren vixen which was giving your chickens such bother. 'Fraid there were rather a lot of people out and those fences away from the Cowpastures took a bit of a hammering. But just to tell you that Tomlin went and repaired the gaps just as soon as the field left your farm, and whilst he was there, he noticed that a couple of your gates needed re-hanging, so he thought he would do that whilst he was there.'

'Captain Wallace, that's very kind indeed.'

'Not at all, Mr Fellows. I hope you are coming to the point-to-point next month. The passes will be round soon and we hope to see you in the Farmers' tent.'

We chuckled at the film because you were almost left with the impression that it was a huge privilege to have the hounds and countless riders over the farm, but, make no mistake, there was a professionalism with the Heythrop Hunt in its dealings with the farming community that did indeed ensure that farmers were properly looked after and given the service they deserve. Inevitably, almost nowhere were the hounds banned.

## Those who were the greatest influence on REW

Five Hunt Servants and two other Masters of hounds made an indelible impression on Ronnie:

- His Eton kennel huntsman Bill Perkins: Ronnie considered that he learned more about Hound Control from him than anyone. I quote: 'Perkins could impart (hound control) to the young in such a way that they could take the pack alone through Slough'.
- George Knight, his k-h at the Ludlow and the Cotswold. Ronnie became great friends with and greatly admired him.
- Will Freeman, from the Eridge, where Ronnie often went in his boyhood.
- Jack Stallard, k-h of the Hawkstone, who looked after hounds for years with virtually no supervision.
- And, of course, dear Percy Durno, from the Heythrop, represented by Nellie, today. (I should add that he thought a great deal of George Gillson, too, from the Warwickshire.)

The two Masters were:

- Sir Peter Farquhar: always a great mentor of Ronnie, mainly because of Sir Peter's immense knowledge and contribution to the breeding and handling of foxhounds in the post war period. Peter more than anyone marked Ronnie's card about hounds and set him on the road named 'Quality' in foxhounds.
- Guy Jackson: father of Charmian, who is here today. Guy was a major influence on his life. He was King of Exmoor, Field Master of the Devon and Somerset before the war. He lost both legs, but became Master of the Exmoor in 1946. It was Guy Jackson who invited Ronnie to take the Cotswold to Exmoor in the spring and so started the annual visit which became known as the Heythrop holiday in later years. Ronnie loved Exmoor

13

and the people and he had always planned to finish his days hunting hounds there. He showed tremendous sport on Exmoor and visitors flocked down each spring and autumn.

Ronnie had great respect also for Master, the tenth Duke of Beaufort and that great Master, amateur huntsman and hound breeder, Bill Scott.

## Ronnie and amateur huntsmen

There must be some fifty or sixty of us, Masters or ex-Masters, who since the war, hunted hounds and had our careers shaped by Ronnie. Some are no longer living. To say that he set the standard is an understatement: We attempted to hunt hounds like him, with varying degrees of success I should say; we tried to organize our country like he did at the Heythrop; we bred our hounds using his lines; we tied our stocks like he did; we blew our horns like mini Wallaces; we tried to sound like him out hunting, and even when we were not out hunting we used his expressions!

Many of us started our hunting lives in total terror of him, and then as the years passed, became friends, and even close friends with him. Why did he have such a hold over us? Without question because we knew and saw that his methods were right. The more we stuck to his pattern, the better we got on. His effect on us undoubtedly compounded his influence over foxhunting throughout the second half of the twentieth century.

It was as if a large number of mini Wallaces had been released to weave their own individual webs. Because he practised high standards and professionalism in the hunting of a pack of hounds and in the organization of countries, we became caught up with those qualities too. And thus the whole performance and presentation of hunting was raised to new heights in many countries.

He was greatly respected by many famous names from the Fell packs. This respect was mutual. He also took immense trouble with Beaglers, always attending beagle day at Peterborough. He was a trustee of the Christchurch and the Eton packs. The annual visit by the Eton to Ronnie and Rosie's Exmoor home, Mounsey, was the highlight of their year.

## Ronnie and hunt staff

If he had huge influence over Masters, his contribution to the lives of so many hunt staff was even greater. He was a brilliant judge of who had the qualities to make a good huntsman or kennel-huntsman. Generations of young men found themselves in the Heythrop stables as second horsemen, before becoming second whip. Many are now senior huntsmen. (It is perhaps as well that minimum wage regulations only appeared late in Ronnie's life, for there was never anything exciting about the wage packet!)

All of these men will have had to bear the Wallace treatment in the field, and perhaps in kennel, but it never broke anyone that I am aware of. It did create a vital regiment of Wallace trained Hunt Staff of immense stature and quality. Without doubt the very high standard of men, possibly at its peak in the 1980s to the end of the last century, was due to Ronnie. He was deeply grateful to the men who were his kennel huntsmen over the years in succession to Percy Durno: Bill Lander, Tony Collins, Anthony Adams and Tony Wright.

## Ronnie the hound breeder

For over fifty years Ronnie was one of the principal hound breeders in the country. History and discussions over the port will doubtless fail to come up with a clear answer as to which hound that he bred was the greatest. However, his own comment was that the Heythrop Brigand '54 male line was his favourite, exemplified by Craftsman '62, Brigand's son. His next favourite line was that of Exmoor Hackler '78, whose forebear was Sir Peter's Portman Wizard '55.

Those of us who have sat year by year on the edge of the ring at Peterborough have seen Ronnie's hounds get ever more classic quality in appearance: Hackler's sons Freestone and Friar were perhaps very close to his best ever. But the influence of Heythrop and Exmoor sires, so many originating from Farquhar bred lines, cleverly crossed to bring in fresh blood, left a mark of quality and scope on hounds in kennels right across Britain and, indeed in Ireland and America.

## Scotland

I must not forget Scotland and The Stalking. Ronnie and Rosie were regular guests of the Flemings at Blackmount and Glen Kinglas. He loved his time on The Hill and made it part of his autumn for years.

## The memories

Each of us has countless memories of this incomparable genius. What he said to us, what we saw him do, the speeches he made, his charismatic and statesmanlike presence at occasions like the

An annual summer treat for R.E.W. – deer stalking in Scotland.

MFHA AGM. But there is a side of Ronnie that not all knew so well: a quality that grew even faster as he grew older, in addition to his immense care and love of people, a special care for those in any kind of difficulty, and those who were dying. He must have spoken at more funerals than any layman I can think of, and he always did it so well because he wanted people to have the very best send off.

He could not have been very easy to have been married to. A few tried and retired. Rosie was married to him for approaching forty years, coping with the endless telephone calls, the constant house guests and Ronnie's regular absence on business. Rosie, you have our love and respect for the great part that you have played in Ronnie's life and for the home and upbringing you have given David.

Ronnie was a Christian, and he believed and trusted in God. He knew that all of us are accountable before God and, if the arrangements for this service are anything to go by, he will have been as prepared for death as much as any of us can be.

Today, our memories are, thankfully, a great deal more eloquent than words. We give heartfelt thanks for this immense and great person; for all the contact we had with him, and for what he gave us. We commend him into the arms of his Maker with the words of Sir Thomas More: 'Pray for us as we will pray for you, that we may meet merrily in heaven'.

# CHAPTER 1

# 'CONVERSATION WITH A MASTER'

The following interview was given to me by Ronnie Wallace for my first foxhunting book, *A Hunting We Will Go*, published in 1967. At that time the effect of urbanization on British hunting countries was far less than would be wrought by the end of the century. There was a good deal of high-class hunting in countries which have nowadays shrunk, or have been amalgamated with their neighbours. Newcomers to the hunting field were arriving each season and Wallace had every reason to be pleased with the huge support and enthusiasm he had evoked in the Heythrop country where he was at the height of his great career.

During two decades since the war he had achieved a remarkable reputation as a huntsman and hound breeder well beyond his own hunting country. In this interview, it was evident that he had thought a great deal about his sport, and its future, and was able to express his views with clarity and vision.

Although optimistic that it would survive, he conceded: 'I don't think you can imagine that changes that are going to happen in the English countryside are going to be very much in favour of hunting.'

However, the constructive view he took of his sport, as conveyed in this interview, gives a clue as to how he was able to encourage so many young men to regard hunting as a worthwhile way of life in the countryside, with a viable future.

*Clayton:* Generally speaking, do you find that a smaller percentage of mounted followers know anything about hunting itself nowadays, and that most people come out simply for the ride?

*Captain Wallace:* It's always been the case that more people come

18

Capt. Ronnie Wallace and his wife Rosie with the Exmoor hounds at a meet at Exford in 1982.

out for the ride than to see hounds work. But I think there are more people interested in hunting itself than before the war because the riding available in a lot of countries isn't quite so good as it was. I think a lot of people are very keen on the hounds now; before the war jolly few people knew what the hounds had done during a day, or had anything to do with them. Broadly, that's as it should be. The whole point of hunting is that people should be able to come out for a hundred different reasons.

But if you ask say twenty people coming home from a day's hunting whether the Heythrop have caught a fox, or how many foxes they have caught, they might say six, they might say one, or they might say none, but I shouldn't think most of them would know.

There are places where people *do* know a lot about hunting because they don't have to bother about jumping fences – areas such as the Fells or on Exmoor.

On Exmoor for example you will see shepherds sitting on the hillsides – and it's no good you trying to tell them what you've done during a day's hunting, because they know better than you do! They are interested in hunting for hunting's sake.

But here, if the huntsman goes out for dinner in the evening people want him to tell them what has actually happened. They are extremely interested, but many tend to look at the sport from the point of view of themselves and their horses. And this is entirely good and natural.

*Clayton:* Do you think it is even more important nowadays to have a really strong Field Master to control the field?

*Wallace:* Yes, I do. One of the main requirements of the Field Master is that he must know whose land he is on. Farmers are still extremely good to the hunt, but quite understandably one farmer will have a sort of fetish about one particular thing which he doesn't want mounted people to do on his land; he might not mind you riding on his corn as long as you don't go into the field where he has got some sheep; another farmer may not mind what you do.

The Field Master has got to have that sort of local knowledge as well as doing his best to ensure that people don't do any damage.

*Clayton:* Turning to the huntsman's role, is there often a conflict of interests in a huntsman's mind in providing a good run for the benefit of the field, and yet allowing his hounds to hunt on slowly if necessary? in other words, should he spend considerable time trying to recover the line of a fox when hounds are at fault, or canter on to the next covert to find another fox quickly?

*Wallace:* The truth lies between the two. In the old days a moderate professional huntsman was too much on the gallop, too apt to lift his hounds as you have described. But there were some perfectly appalling amateurs who would just sit, hounds having checked in a field of sheep or something like that. Such a huntsman might sit for twenty minutes waiting to see what had happened and then make a walking cast round the same field. We have all seen that – and it *is* appalling.

This is why Major Hilton-Green* was such a wonderful huntsman because he hunted the fox with his hounds and at the same time he could keep several hundred very well mounted horsemen at bay.

The huntsman does not want to spoil his hounds; he wants to catch his fox. But at the same time it is not any good sitting about, because many people come out to gallop and jump.

The excitement of foxhunting is the 'hooroosh of the chase'.

---

* Major C. C. Hilton-Green was amateur huntsman of the Cottesmore from 1931–46.

You get your slow bit of hunting but it shouldn't fizzle out every time. On a great many occasions you should work up to your fox and get going again.

Technically, the thing that should always be in the huntsman's mind is never to waste a second. Hounds may check on a big area of plough because they have got a little bit behind, or because the scent isn't lying too well on the plough that day, or possibly because the fox has turned short.

Under those circumstances you are not wasting time by waiting to see what hounds are doing; if your hounds are trying, and hunting sensibly they are going to show you the line before you can cast them.

*Clayton:* Presumably the modern foxhound also has to ensure that he doesn't waste a second?

*Wallace:* A foxhound must be quick to react. It's this bit that counts (Captain Wallace tapped his head and grinned). The Badminton and the Portman blood is what has helped our hounds.

The conformation of the foxhound today is such that he can gallop easily and doesn't tire and this gives him the ability to have good fox-sense.

You can develop your hounds to a pitch where it is immediately apparent if something does go wrong in the pack. They will check and do things which couldn't possibly be right; there is one hound putting them wrong. You have then got to worry like anything, and until you get rid of that element you are in a jam.

You have got to hunt on terms with the fox on farming land today. If you go down to the wilds of the west you can still hunt a fox that has been gone half an hour or three-quarters of an hour before.

But hunting on terms with the fox means that a hound has got to keep the pressure up, and he's got to hunt terribly accurately. It is no good him sliding on another hundred yards beyond where he has got the scent. He has got to go like the devil and jam the brakes on to turn quickly, so that he can keep close to the fox.

Nowadays you can't hunt what I call 'by and large'; perhaps in the old grass countries they fizzed along and the fox turned to the left, and the hounds went on a bit; the huntsman picked them up and he made a good sweep round and hit it off.

Today you have got to say to hounds: 'No, no, no, you're wrong here. The fox hasn't gone *that* side of the gateway, he's gone *this* side.' You must stand still, and make them do it. Otherwise you get off the line, you've got other difficulties in the next field, perhaps more plough or sheep, and you are in trouble.

*Clayton:* Getting hounds out of covert quickly must be even more important nowadays than ever it was?

*Wallace:* Yes, it's a frightfully important thing. You must get away quickly. You want a good staff. Preventing the pack splitting is good staff work.

*Clayton:* Where do you post your whippers-in when you go into covert?

*Wallace:* Oh, I send them on. I don't have a whipper-in with me very often. We certainly don't go in for what I call 'dog wallopers'.

*Clayton:* You use whistles in the Heythrop for communication between hunt staff, but are members of the field discouraged from holloa-ing?

*Wallace:* I don't mind holloa-ing. I think everybody enjoys it. After all, it's better to proclaim that you have seen a fox than keeping it secret and only saying so the next day!

*Clayton:* Do you find that foxes will cross roads in your country?

*Wallace:* Oh yes, they don't take the slightest notice. Foxes are modern animals; they know it's 1967 just as much as we do.

*Clayton:* But don't you find that modern roads cause more foxes to be headed and prevent points being achieved?

*Wallace:* It's absolutely no good giving in, and assuming that you are only going to get local hunting. If you have this in your mind when you go out, then local hunting is what you will get. In a country such as this, where we have big mounted fields, foxes do run much straighter.

But when you are hunting with a lot of people following, foil is a tremendous problem, and I always hate it if we run back. It is hopeless in a country like ours or the Duke of Beaufort's if you keep running back into the foil of the horses. You are absolutely done.

If the fox runs along a route where the riders have all been in the morning it's got to be an exceptional scenting day for hounds to run through that. You have got so much ground which you can't account for, if you are casting under those conditions.

If you are lucky you can overcome it, but it's a little bit by guess work. Foil of horses is almost worse than any other foil.

If you ran back tomorrow into the country you were hunting today you'd be awfully annoyed if you were still stopped by the foil you had left. Whereas if you ran back at four o'clock in the afternoon to the place where you had been at eleven-thirty in the morning you would *expect* to be stopped.

I'd love to know at what point the scent of foil disappears. Do you think it disappears in the night air, or what?

*Clayton:* Could we turn to some of the outside influences which may affect hunting? For example, what is your view about the clash of interest between hunting and a strong shooting interest in a country?

*Wallace:* I don't think there is much difficulty over shooting provided that the people who run shoots will control their own keepers. The mistake is to leave it to the gamekeeper and merely say there's got to be 'a fox' when hounds come to the covert. One fox is about as much good as ten pheasants on a shooting day because he may not be there, or he may disappear the second you find him, or he may be stopped in. Provided the 'keeper understands it is just as much his duty to provide proper sport for the hunting as for the shooting, then all will be well.

I don't think you can expect a gamekeeper on a shooting establishment, where his employer perhaps isn't as keen on hunting as shooting, to keep every fox . . . but the trouble is that some gamekeepers today are not really countrymen and they don't know how the balance of nature operates.

*Clayton:* Presumably, it is very important indeed for Masters to maintain good liaison with all covert owners so that they are really aware of what is best for the hunt?

*Wallace:* This is true, and fortunately there are some wonderful 'keepers; we've got some in this country. But nowadays it is up to hunting people to protect important coverts by taking the shooting themselves if necessary. I don't think it is any good leaving these matters to chance.

*Clayton:* Plough is a growing problem in many countries nowadays. How much plough do you have in the Heythrop country, and how do you tackle the problem?

*Wallace:* By February, more than fifty per cent of our country is plough. Between the wars there was some plough here, and in a lot of other countries there was very little plough at all. Years before that, there was probably as much plough as there is now. But in the past, farming methods weren't quite so ruthless and ploughing was done much more slowly; a lot of the stubbles weren't ploughed until February, and many fields were left fallow. Now every corner is ploughed out, and if there's a hedge or a wall in the way there's tendency to say 'Let's get a bulldozer and push it out.'

*Clayton:* Now that the headlands are ploughed out, it must be difficult to use the old technique of picking up the line where the fox had come through a fence, judging the direction it had taken across a field, and then picking up the line on the headland on the other side of the field?

*Wallace:* Yes, that's what we used to call 'smeusing'. Well, for one thing, hounds get used to crossing plough, and sometimes hounds run faster on the plough than they do on the grass where there are a lot of sheep. The last two seasons have been good scenting ones and our hounds fly across the ploughs; sometimes you can't live with them.

Of course, we are lucky in that we have pretty light land in our country. In some countries the plough seems almost bottomless and you can't jump fences from it, whereas in this country you can often pop over a wall.

We have 'put it about' in the country that it is a great help to leave the headlands unploughed, even just a plough's width, until, say February when cultivations are starting. Fortunately, we get a great deal of co-operation – and it's terribly useful, because everyone out hunting uses the headland, including the fox, which is most important.

*Clayton:* So, for all these reasons you don't find plough much of a problem?

*Wallace:* Oh, no. Certainly not.

*Clayton:* Are you reasonably optimistic about the future of foxhunting?

*Wallace:* Oh yes, I don't think you can imagine that changes that are going to happen in the English countryside are going to be very much in favour of hunting. But despite all the difficulties, we have managed quite well so far, and there is a tremendous feeling for the sport still in the countryside, and in the towns as well.

One of the big difficulties is to know how you are going to cope with the numbers who would like to take part in our country sports. What the solution is, I simply don't know. I am sure hunting will continue to flourish, but I think there will not be quite so many little hunts in the future. I think the new motor-ways will necessitate the reorganization of hunting countries. Amalgamation of hunts is going to occur more frequently in the next five to ten years.

*Clayton:* This is a reversion to the old days when hunting countries were much bigger?

*Wallace:* Yes, it is. In some cases, the very small hunts are hunting inadequate areas at present. Amalgamation would also make sense on economic grounds. If you are using only one hunting establishment it does not cost twice as much to hunt four days a week instead of two – not quite. Whereas it costs *more* than twice as much if you have two separate establishments each hunting two days a week.

*Clayton:* What are the future prospects for professional huntsmen?

*Wallace:* I think the outlook for professionals is good. There are some wonderful men in the profession, and the younger generation has rather taken over in many places in the last five years.

Some of the old professionals seem to think that their trade is being taken over everywhere by amateurs, but this is not so – there were always a lot of amateur huntsmen and there may be one in a country where a professional was traditionally employed. But the reverse occurs as well, and I do not foresee a first-class huntsman or kennel huntsman being short of a place.

# CHAPTER 2

# How to Breed
# a Pack of Foxhounds

By the end of the twentieth century it was accepted throughout the hunting world that Ronnie Wallace had played a vital role in raising the standard of England Foxhound breeding.

Not only was his influence crucial in the British Isles, but a significant number of North American packs were using his lines, and he regularly judged hounds at the major US shows.

As he explains below, he did not favour using Welsh outcrosses in his own hounds, but he was not at all prejudiced against Welsh hounds in general. He felt, however, that there had already been enough Welsh outcrosses used in English kennels earlier in the twentieth century, and it was not wise to tip the balance further.

His own outcrosses were American, West Country Harrier, Fell and Old English. A great admirer of Wallace hound breeding, Martin Scott, who had been so successful as a hound breeder at the VWH, has written: 'The American crosses have introduced completely new lines, and have brought nose, tongue and keenness. Orange County Barber '89 and Live Oak Drummer '89 brought in new top lines which have yet to prove themselves here. Old Dominion Gorgeous '68 brought in a new female line that is now established. The Captain admired William Brainard, who produced Gorgeous. Of Fell blood, he said: "The trouble with the Fell is that, as they get older, they become a bit more cunning." Even so, he preferred this outcross to the Welsh.'

Wallace enjoyed winning rosettes at shows, and bred thirty-three Peterborough champions, but he never lost sight of the real aim in hound breeding – hounds that hunt well in the field. He would remark that his greatest satisfaction was in achieving that aim.

Martin Scott noted Ronnie Wallace's policy of 'ringing the

changes' which required encyclopaedic knowledge of pedigrees. He recorded that when Wallace left the Cotswold to join the Heythrop Mastership 'he took a good line – Brocklesby Nightshade 1859, with strong Carlow influence, from which came a great favourite, Exmoor Pixie 1986. He also took Ludlow Bangle '46 with him, full of Sir Edward Rouse Boughton's good lines going back to Sir Watkin Williams-Wynn's Prosperine 1843. Bangle was dam of the influential Brigand '54. She hunted into her tenth season – longevity was another quality the Captain admired.

'He was a great strategist, using trusted friends to introduce female lines – one from the South Dorset which produced the S line at the Heythrop, and one from the Kilkenny. Both these female lines also trace back tail female to Sir Thomas Mostyn's Lady 1801. He acquired my father's (Major Bill Scott) female line, bought from Sir Edward Curre in 1931, which is the female line of Heythrop Berry '78, and their recent champion, Chorus 2000. Wallace said: "I valued the Brigand '54 line especially. Craftsman sixty-two was his best son." Asked to name his next best line, he said: Exmoor Hackler '78, by Heythrop Grossmith '71, a great hound. He came through a Portman grey hound called Portman Wizard '55. One day I saw Hackler jump a wall and wind a fox in a big bramble bush, and he jumped straight on top of the bush.'

Four ingredients make up the successful conduct of foxhunting. The first is organization, which covers every aspect of the Master's arrangements, and without that you get nowhere. The second ingredient is the skill of the Hunt staff. The third ingredient is a well-bred and efficient pack of hounds. And the fourth is a little bit of extra woodcraft and venery on the part of the huntsman.

The reason that the hounds are the third ingredient and not the second is because a good pack of hounds can be ruined by bad handling, whereas a good handler can contrive the sport with a scratch pack of hounds.

Some of your readers might say that the breeding and production of a fine pack of hounds is a bit technical, and of most interest to Masters and huntsmen. But when you think that the emphasis on riding across country in many Hunt territories is not quite what it was years ago – and when you consider the number of people who keenly walk hounds for the local Hunt and attend the puppy show – then I think that what hounds are, and what they do, might be of more interest to a wider selection of people.

When a new Master takes a pack of hounds he will obviously have a good look at what he has taken on. Although in most

The Master during a hunting day with the Exmoor bitch pack.

countries hounds are the property of the Committee, an outgoing Master is entitled in nearly all cases to take the surplus away and give them to friends. The ingoing Master may think that the hounds that are left are not quite what he wants. But the criminal thing for him to do is to get rid of a great many of the native pack until he has got himself firmly in the saddle. The man who comes along and destroys years of careful breeding by giving the hounds away because he thinks they are not good enough is doing the Hunt a disservice.

Ultimately, to get a pack you want a type. It may take a little time to achieve this. But when you have a type it is very bad work then to get rid of that type without great excuse.

The first thing for the new Master to do is to trace the tail female line – the dam right back to the Ark; we can trace hounds back to the late eighteenth century quite easily and in some cases a bit further. If he concentrates, and finds out what tail female lines he has, then he can look round for doghounds of the type to suit him.

Having several female lines increases the options. It is perfectly legitimate, if a Master intends to remain in the country, to introduced extra female lines as long as the inherent Kennel lines, if they exist, are not destroyed. If this has already happened, the new Master must do his best according to his taste. One cannot be confident of achieving anything from a mating of hounds. Yet, just as a child at a Christmas party can get nothing from the bran tub that was not put into it in the first place, so it is with the attributes of hounds. Put them in the tub and some of them will come out. If over many years there has been built up a concentration of the blood you favour, then the chances of getting what you want are increased.

Of course, you can inbreed only to an extent. The more you inbreed, the greater distance you will eventually have to go for the outcross, and you may have to persist with the outcross rather further than you like. Although an outcross is very valuable, in my view it is a mistake to go too far with it. I like to have perhaps two or three litters in an outcross and then try to integrate them back into the Kennel type. If the blood lines are strong enough, they come to your type straight away. At the Duke of Beaufort's Kennel all sorts of unusual hounds can be used, as the late Duke used to do, but his strength and stamina and type came through very fast.

One of the difficulties now – and some of us must take a responsibility for this – is that packs of hounds have become much more similar, one to another, whereas years ago there were family packs of quite different sorts. Take the Beaufort, Fitzwilliam, Brocklesby and the Belvoir; the two latter, with the Hurworth, the South York and Ainsty, to some extent the Limerick, Muskerry and Co Waterford, still stick to what is now called the Old English lines, and long may they flourish, because they have great intrinsic value.

It was unfashionable in, say, 1930 to go against that type whereas, led by Isaac Bell of immortal memory, and supported by the Duke of Beaufort, Peter Farquhar, Bill Scott, George Coventry, Jack Evans and others, the hound which is fashionable today has emerged. I think one of the most influential people in the story of the foxhound has been Peter Farquhar, during his Masterships of the Tedworth, Meynell and of the Whaddon Chase before the war, and then of course the Portman, at a vital time just after the war when hounds had to be built up again. He set an example by producing some excellent doghounds.

One characteristic of a good hound breeder is that he is suspicious. I would never use a dog, no matter how nice he was as an

Heythrop Rocket ('61), Peterborough Royal Foxhound Show bitch champion in 1962.

individual, from a Kennel which I did not think was tip-top, unless it was some blood of ours that I wanted to get back.

I have watched people hasten to use a certain doghound which I know to be a smart one from a pack that does not ordinarily produce good hounds. The Duke of Beaufort once told me – and I quote him because it sounds a remarkable observation – that the pedigree of the huntsman or Master is almost as important as the pedigree of the hound. When you are breeding back to famous hounds of the past, it is well to remember that.

So when the tyro Master is looking for doghounds, do not let him be misled by the chance-bred hound recommended by a huntsman who happens to have a dog of which he is fond, and for which he would like some nice wives. Let him get out to the place where the most sport is shown and the most foxes caught.

Where to go now is not easy. There are too few Kennels with any variety of doghounds, and we have reached the stage where our hounds are pretty closely bred. Badminton has just been through a slight transition but the efforts of the present Duke and of Captain Ian Farquhar are bearing fruit. The Berkeley have some nice doghounds. Do not forget the Brocklesby, or, for that matter, the Exmoor hounds, which are an extension of the Heythrop!

I was urged years ago to launch out in other directions, which in the last fifteen or sixteen years at the Exmoor we have done. But I did not do it until it was necessary. Two major things I have learned: that the tail male and tail female lines are the important elements; and that one should not go mad – dabble a little, see what it is like, then, if you approve, possibly have a bit more.

The first outcross we had of great significance, other than Brocklesby dogs, was thanks to Mr William Brainard from Virginia, who sent me a bitch of his called Old Dominion Gorgeous. We have got a dynasty here now, of which Gladness was champion hound at Peterborough the year before last and typifies what we are getting. Their nose and tongue is notable still through the generations.

Then I have had an excellent female line from the Eskdale and Ennerdale; a male line of the West Country Harriers of which I am hopeful, from a dog, Taunton Vale Catlow, which gets his West Country breeding through the Cotley, and from which I am hoping there will be a dynasty. I have not gone again to Wales.

Some say that I am prejudiced against the Welsh hound; not true. Quite simply, I have seen English Kennels where they have had too much Welsh blood, and it has upset the balance of the pack. Among the great hound men of Wales at one time were Jack Evans at the Brecon, Lord Coventry at the Carmarthenshire and Lord Davies at the David Davies. They were all experts, and they blended the Welsh blood with the best of the English. Of them, only Lord Davies remains as upholder of a family pack.

When the young Master starts breeding, by spreading the net fairly wide, it does not pay to then narrow it again too quickly. Many people breed a decent hound or two and think they are home and dry. They go back to their own inbreeding and in a year or two they are back to square one. Although we bred two Peterborough champions in the first four years at the Heythrop Kennels – good foxhounds too – we were still going for outcrosses.

I have said that one of the sins is to get rid of inherited hounds without finding out what they are. The other criminal offence is to keep a hound that is not great for hunting because it might win a prize or has won a prize. Hounds should be good hunters, which cannot be easy in some countries. One does come across people – I am glad to say not many – who might be tempted to do this, and it is the reverse side of the good which hound shows may do.

Hound shows are excellent for showing people what hounds are about. They are a great incentive to puppy walkers, to Masters to breed, and to huntsmen to see what is required. But in these days when some hunting countries are not as good as they were, the temptation could be there to breed for show. On the whole, the packs which seem to win the most prizes at the hound shows are the ones which catch the most foxes. Long may that prevail.

At my time of life, the breeding of the hounds becomes the most fascinating part of the job. It is the one that motivates. But you can overdo the hound-fancying, the theories and the fashion. I have always been one for showing sport. That is my job.

## Hound Talk with the Master

In 1994 I interviewed Ronnie Wallace in depth on his views on modern hound breeding, and the direction it was taking. He deals with the controversial subject of Welsh breeding in more detail, and recounts an incident he had with a Welsh draft hound while he was hunting the

32

Lovely ladies: the Heythrop's winning two couple of bitches at Peterborough in 1961. Clematis ('59) who also won the bitch championship, Fanciful, Chaffinch and Chatty.

Cotswold pack which may go some way to explaining his own antipathy to Welsh outcrosses.

He tells of his successful usage of other outcrosses, including American lines such as the Orange County and Old Dominion.

*Question:* Do you think hound shows are useful, or largely a fashion show, since hounds are really bred for work?
*Answer:* The value of the hound shows is untold, provided you understand that work always comes first. It is not only helpful to see what hounds other people have got, and how you can improve yours, but at a show you can see a type, which perhaps makes it easier to get your own hounds together at home.

I think that another important thing is that it is quite thrilling

for the puppy walkers. It helps to make them feel there is something to aim for, and it is good that important prizes are given to
puppy walkers at the hound shows nowadays.

The danger of hound shows lies in encouraging a Master to
think: 'We'd better keep that hound because it won a prize at such
and such a show . . .' Of course, a doghound which has won a
major championship can have a lot of bitches sent to him from
other kennels. It is very important that the offspring are then
judged solely on their work before this line becomes too popular.
We must not have too many hound shows, either.

Q: What should be the attitude towards hound breeding by a
Master who has taken on a new country?

A: Most packs have existed for a long time and hopefully they
have been bred to hunt their own particular countries. It is all too
easy to lose a valuable line for ever if the wrong decisions are
taken hastily.

One must assess what you have in the kennel and it may be that
there are problems to be addressed. First, work out and assess the
female lines you have. Of course, action can be taken to introduce
some appropriate new lines, but nothing drastic should be
attempted unless the new Master is pretty sure he, or she, is
staying in office for some seasons to come.

One knows of a few Hunts where the actions of certain Masters
have been almost criminal in emptying kennels of what has been
there for a long time and had been very acceptable to people
hunting regularly in those countries. Certain packs which were
of high repute have lost the essential core of the breeding which
had achieved so much.

Q: What about new outcrosses: How has the Duke of Beaufort's
managed to absorb so much new Welsh blood so successfully?

A: Master [the 10th Duke] had such strong lines in the kennel.
When he was a young man he did a lot of work on hound
breeding which involved introducing Welsh blood and therefore
the latest outcrosses have nicked in well.

Much of the pioneering between the wars in outcross hound
breeding was achieved by Ikey Bell [the American born MFH and
amateur huntsman, whose Mastership of the South and West
Wilts was especially notable for innovative hound breeding].

Master once told me he used to be worried about his
traditionally-bred hounds tailing off in the hunting field. One of
the great virtues of the Ikey Bell sort of hound was that they
caught up.

A very discerning man, who was a car follower, said to me when I first went to the Cotswold: 'When I see your new pack run up together quick I'll know you're some good.'

The great advantage in trying the original Welsh outcrosses was the influence of great hound breeding experts in Wales between the wars.

There was Sir Edward Curre who sadly died in 1930; perhaps the greatest hound expert of the lot, George, Earl of Coventry who was Master of the Carmarthenshire and was killed at Dunkirk; Lord Davies of the David Davies and there was Captain Jack Evans of the Brecon, a fine breeder, whose brother was secretary of the Ludlow when I went there [in 1944].

In those days, there wasn't too much Welsh blood in packs outside Wales. I remember just after the war, Bert Buckley, who was a good hound man and took over from Lord Coventry at the Carmarthenshire, said to me: 'You must try this hound . . .' It was a huge Welsh doghound, named Abraham, like an enormous red fox, from the Pantysgallog pack.

I hunted him with the Cotswold pack on a very good scenting morning at a lovely place called Miserden, where the Wills family live. We had a marvellous morning's cubhunting, with valleys to cross and no 'Tally Ho back'.

We caught a brace of foxes, and the red hound was prominent in all.

Next morning we went to Colonel Elwes's Hillcote Wood. It was a muggy morning, very bad scenting; hounds found a fox and ran up the wood.

That was about all we did all the morning, but the Welsh hound went back on the heel line – like an Otterhound – and when he got to where they had found the fox, he went back again on the line. The others soon lost their enthusiasm and the Pantysgallog hound went back to Wales after that!

Bert Buckley said: 'Well now you've learned something!'

I wouldn't want to make too much of that incident, but it was rather an interesting example of a problem you can have with outcrosses.

Q: Well, you have not joined in the postwar use of Welsh sires in your own hound breeding. As you say, there was already Welsh blood in the so-called modern hound, brought in between the wars. But you have used other outcrosses with success. Some people have been known to use the odd Harrier line with their Foxhounds; have you done this?

*A:* Yes, I've got a West Country Harrier line, a male line which is tenuous at present. There is only one tail male line which is West Country Harrier and there is a lot of Foxhound blood in the pedigree. The Cotley and other Harrier packs have of course hunted the fox for a long time. It was sometimes though that this Harrier was of great value in an enclosed country. They are very good fox catchers because they can turn short. My line was from a Taunton Vale Harriers doghound, going back to the Cotley via Axe Vale. This hound went to Ben Hardaway's Midland pack in Georgia, USA, and the last time I saw the hound was in Canada.

*Q:* The Cotley was recognized by the MFHA in 1948, but I believe the *Foxhound Kennel Stud Book* was closed to Harriers and others at that time?

*A:* Absolutely. In 1928, the *Foxhound Kennel Stud Book* was 'closed' to hounds not bred, entered and worked in recognized Foxhound kennels.

This excluded many of the Welsh and others. After the war there was a furious debate about this and eventually the *Stud Book* was opened again to many packs which had been debarred, but had been producing sport by hunting foxes. This was due mainly to the far-sightedness of Sir Peter Farquhar, 'Mo' Barclay, and Master.

In 1955, it was ruled that it was only necessary to prove that hounds had pedigrees going back five generations, later increased to six, to ancestors kept for hunting only the fox and that they came from established packs of Foxhounds which had been hunting the fox only for at least ten years. These packs are entered in a section at the back of the *Stud Book*.

It is pre-supposed that Masters of Foxhounds can actually read and, after all, the *Stud Book* is only a list of hounds. As a Master you must make your own hound breeding decisions, aided by the information you can glean from experienced people in this field.

*Q:* Opening the Stud Book must have been a sensible decision since so much Welsh blood had been introduced into English packs by then. And the original, so-called pure English hound could not really have been entirely of the type which its critics referred to as the 'Shorthorn' because of its heavy build. There must have been a lot of variations in type within the English hound still hunted widely well into this century?

*A:* Frank Freeman, for example, did not hunt big, heavily-built hounds in his tremendously successful English-bred pack at the Pytchley. He made his name by acquiring and hunting a pack of little bitches, quite a lot of them purchased at the old Rugby Hound Sale.

There was a famous story that one of the hound experts of the day, the Rev Cecil Legard, saw the Pytchley hounds at the meet at Daventry in 1911. As he turned away, he remarked: 'Pack of harriers.' The meet was followed by the famous Badby Wood run in which hounds achieved a fourteen-mile point, running about twenty-two miles and catching their fox.

On Sunday morning, Legard came to the kennels, and said: 'Freeman, you had a great hunt.' Freeman replied: 'Yes sir. Not bad for harriers.'

I knew Frank Freeman's brother, Will, very well, and he got his Masters to acquire little 'slippy' hounds from Kilkenny when I was a boy in the Eridge country. Of course, they were quite quick enough for Sussex and were gone all too quickly in the hunting field! They were marvellous.

I always remember asking him about hunting Welsh-cross hounds.

He said: 'Yes, they hunt very well. Trouble is they get too much of it and then they have three packs out on the same day.' That is the danger, but we must be fair and say that Welsh blood properly introduced, and with a pack well-handled, has produced remarkably good hunting hounds.

If you want to have a really good pack of hounds, you must try an outcross carefully and then integrate it with yours. There are other people who just like experimenting. They have a great many hounds and just get rid of those which are failures in their work.

Q: The key to consistent hound breeding is surely the production of great stallion hounds of a consistent type?

A: When I arrived at Heythrop I was able to reap the benefit of using the same excellent bloodlines from their kennel. We had an important male line which I was able to develop from Sergeant ('46) who went back to Heythrop Carver ('38) and thus from Chorister ('06), Warwickshire in the last century, then the best.

I believed it to be the best male line in the stud book, and in 1954 we bred Heythrop Brigand, by Sergeant. Brigand turned out to be extremely influential.

When the Farquhars and the Beauforts were looking around for a fresh sire, they suddenly found Brigand who practically had a virgin pedigree; he filled the gap. Some people said it was very

Portman Wizard ('55) by Sailor ('52). A very influential sire, bred by Lt. Col. Sir Peter Farquhar. Wizard descended from the great Heythrop Chorister ('06)

Heythrop Brigand ('54) by Sergeant('46) out of Ludlow Bangle ('46), one of the most influential and extensively used sires of the mid-century, descending in tail male from Heythrop Carver ('38)

Heythrop Harper ('53) by Portman Lovelock ('47) out of Cotswold Handcuff ('49), the first hound from this kennel to win a Peterborough championship. He was stallion hound winner and doghound champion in 1955.

Heythrop Blackcock ('59), son of Portman Wizard, Peterborough doghound champion in 1961, and proved an outstanding worker.

Heythrop Desert ('72), Peterborough bitch champion in 1974.

Heythrop Craftsman ('62) by Brigand ('54) out of Crystal ('59). Craftsman was Peterborough doghound champion in 1962 and also won the stallion hound class.

Exmoor Fortescue ('77), by Meynell and S. Staffs Growler ('74) out of Heythrop Flicker ('75), winner of the 1980 Peterborough bitch championship.

Exmoor Daresbury ('87), by Berkeley David ('81) out of Dusty ('84), Peterborough doghound champion, 1990.

Exmoor Pixie ('86) by Duke of Beaufort's Pickwick ('82) out of Redcap ('82), Peterborough bitch champion in 1987.

Heythrop Cardinal ('63) by Craftsman ('62) out of Chatty ('62), winner as an unentered hound of Peterborough doghound championship in 1964.

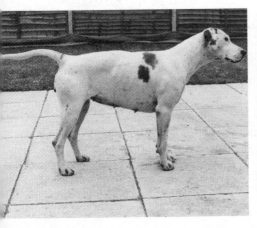

doubtful because there were things that had not been heard of in the female line, but look where it has got us since.

It has proved to be a great line and the recipient at the moment is a hound called Exmoor Daresbury.

Q: Did you consciously change the type of your hounds at all when you moved from the Heythrop to hunt the moorland country of the Exmoor?

A: Not at all; same thing. They have simply evolved, as all packs of hounds must. Mind you, it is much more difficult to win major prizes at the hound shows nowadays because so many more people have become conscious of the successful lines and have used them in their own kennels.

Q: Has foxhound breeding now arrived at a situation where there is a great need for yet another new major outcross?

A: Breeding hounds is an ongoing situation. People of great authority said to me when I was still at the Heythrop that it appeared that I was breeding hounds on orthodox lines and they wanted to know when I was going to launch out with something 'really inventive'. The fact was that the Duke of Beaufort, Peter Farquhar, Peach Borwick and others had already used Welsh blood to alter some very famous packs and they had done it with great discretion.

I was able to reap the benefit of that. The hound breeders I have mentioned above were kind enough to take me under their wing and I received some excellent hounds from their kennels. Then I arrived at the Heythrop where there was a very well established pack, slightly of a 'good plain cook' type and based on a female line, a branch of Sir Thomas Mostyn's Lady, 1801.

Thanks to the friends I have already mentioned, we were able to upgrade from there, and it was a successful hound breeding policy for more than twenty years. Other people were doing much the same thing.

Occasionally, I would go back to the blood of the Brocklesby which always worked well at the Heythrop. One half-bred Brocklesby bitch called Dabchick apprehended a fox which doubled back in a good hunt on Dartmoor and ran past her when she was hanging upside down from a wire fence! You could hardly have better proof that this breeding produced great hunting hounds.

You ring the changes on your lines, based in my view on the tail male and the tail female lines. Sir Peter Farquhar was kind enough to give me a similar book to one which Ikey Bell gave him, and which was so beautifully compiled by Daphne Moore.

This contained male and female tail lines, and I am among those who attach much importance to them. Then, thanks to my friendship with Edmund Porter, Master of the Eskdale and Ennerdale in the Fells – I used to go out with him and his hounds in the spring – I was able to introduce a Fell line into the Heythrop.

I was standing in a road one day when the Eskdale and Ennerdale hounds came down off the Fells in pursuit of their fox on to the road. I wondered what course of action I would have taken at that moment if I had been on my horse hunting my hounds.

I was immensely impressed when these Fell hounds immediately did what I hoped I would have done. It was a complicated situation because there was a turn in the road, and side roads. They cast themselves brilliantly and quickly picked up the line of the hunted fox – and they did it all on their own.

Heythrop Hedgerow ('71) champion bitch, and brood bitch class winner at Peterborough 1975. She was by West Dulverton Romper ('65) out of Heather ('67).

41

I used an Eskdale and Ennerdale sire called Bendigo and this Fell line has been successful.

When it came to other outcrosses, I had valuable assistance from across the Atlantic. A great friend was the late William Brainard, Master of the Old Dominion, in Virginia.

He was a marvellous judge of almost any animal, and he was very kind in sending me an Old Dominion bitch, named Gorgeous.

She had actually been with Dick Eames at the Cotley first and she had earlier had her nerve shattered because she was kept in quarantine for nine or ten months on arrival from the United States because there had been a scare at Camberley over an imported dog with rabies.

Our Hunt servants did not at all like having her out in the hunting field where she tended to flop along. We were drawing a kale field one morning, and one does not often find a fox going to ground in a kale field, but Gorgeous was marking with great enthusiasm. She had actually found a very nice leaf of kale carrying a strong fox scent and so she was barking at that! This was not a great start, but it did not prevent her later going into a pit covered with brambles, taking several companions with her, and they caught two or three foxes straight away, with other foxes flying in all directions.

She had sixteen puppies in her first litter, but alas they were like mice and died.

But she came into season again in July the same year. We put her to and she had six beautiful puppies, including four bitches, in September.

Bob Field-Marsham at the Eridge had one and Martin Scott, then at the Tiverton, had another, later taking his to the VWH and founding a dynasty there.

I actually kept two and although in their first season they were a bit immature and flat-footed, one hunted eight and the other nine seasons.

They have marvellous noses and distinctive voices. Once when I visited the Eridge one early morning I was able to pick out a bitch speaking in a wood as one of the Old Dominion line because her voice was so similar to that of her sisters at home.

We have had this female line now for eighteen years; it takes a bit of absorbing into our sort, but it has produced some good hounds, including a nice bitch called Gladness which won a championship at Peterborough in 1991 and the brood bitch class last year.

More recently, Bill Brainard arranged for me to acquire an Orange County doghound, named Barber, who has proved successful.

People have asked me why I went to American packs. The answer is that their hounds are not unintelligent, they certainly have excellent noses and voice and are proving to have sufficient stamina. In any case, it was a complete change of blood in the kennel, which is essential at some point.

As I said before, Foxhound breeding is an ongoing process.

*Q:* But when a pack produces consistently good sport, which factor is predominant, the breeding or the handling by the huntsman?

*A:* The breeding is, of course, important, but undoubtedly the major factor is always the way the hounds are handled by the huntsman in the field. But that is another subject . . .

# CHAPTER 3

# BACK FROM WALK – BRINGING ON YOUNG HOUNDS IN THE PACK

Several times I had the privilege of riding out with Ronnie Wallace when he was exercising his hounds before the start of his season on Exmoor.

This happened in July because the opening meets in this beautiful moorland of hills and valleys start in August.

Wallace rode ahead with over thirty couple of older hounds and the new entry. Seen from below they scattered over the heather-clad hill around him in the early morning sunshine like giant seagulls. A whipper-in was riding far out on the flank, but he was not needed to ensure the pack stayed near their huntsman as if held by an invisible thread of leadership and control. Then he rode into some large grass enclosures where flocks of sheep were grazing. He passed very close to the sheep with his hounds. Suddenly he stopped, and called to one hound which he had noticed taking too much interest in some grazing lambs.

Ronnie leaned forward, shook his finger at the hound, and scolded him for a few minutes, but not in a particularly loud voice. It was like a senior prefect telling a junior to behave. I saw the hound's stern droop, and he lay down submissively to receive his verbal chastisement.

Older hounds drew away from the culprit with ex-pressions of horror, almost tut-tutting out loud at this transgression.

'If possible it's much better to catch this sort of thing early and then teach a young hound by voice, and by the dis-approval of the older hounds, than to have to resort to corporal punishment' said Wallace later.

Although he did not regularly take charge of summer hound exercise, leaving it to his kennel huntsman and staff, Wallace's link with his hounds was such that when he

44

arrived at a meet during the season to mount his horse, the pack would crowd round his horse and bay at him. Their main allegiance is not to the man who feeds them, but to he who shows them sport.

Entering his young hounds successfully was a major factor in the quality of sport Ronnie Wallace achieved so consistently throughout a long season.

One of the most exciting sides to a Master's or huntsman's life is the development of a pack of hounds – particularly in cases where things have gone wrong in the past, and the pack needs to be re-shaped. The successful planning of matings from a pedigree and a hunting point of view is one objective, but now we are considering its result.

The development from bundles of charm as puppies to grown hounds ready to hunt depends tremendously on devoted puppy-walkers. The cult of puppy-walking has developed greatly since the war. Although there were a few famous puppy-walkers, sometimes puppies then were kept largely confined. Now that has changed. Puppies live as members of the family, and improvements in worming and inoculations against distemper have helped to create excellent conditions for the rearing of hounds. The devotion of puppy-walkers to their local pack, and their continued interest in the hounds they have walked, surpass admiration.

Care of puppies is just like care of children. Both need some discipline. For hound puppies this need only include answering to their names, basic instructions, and if possible, going comparatively willingly on a collar and lead. After that all depends on love, as with children. Young hounds who are given genuine interest and love are the ones that flourish all their lives.

Puppies which hunt a lot at walk can have an advantage over those which do not. Nevertheless, those which have not been encouraged or allowed to hunt by their walkers can be the quickest to enter in the autumn. I remember one place years ago where a walker used to take the hound puppies out and deliberately hunt them. Those which came back from that particular walk could be very headstrong.

Hound puppies, known as 'the young 'uns', come back into kennels at any time from November until April or May, depending on their age. Some puppy-walkers are so keen on their charges that we can hardly prise them apart until we produce substitutes, which is rather nice. When at last the puppies arrive at the kennels, they are like schoolboys at boarding school for the first time. Some do not give a damn, others are shy. A day or two later the penny drops. They become part of the pack and no longer individuals singly loved. Settling in depends then on the huntsman and the kennelman. They must be nice to the young hounds, but firm.

The youngsters go straight in with the older hounds, except for any which are shy or upset. They will be kennelled on their own, or with one or two others, to start with. Young hounds are fed in the same way as the rest. In the old days, oatmeal was the staple diet, and in the summer it was mixed with flaked maize and rice, but that was in more palmy times. Some people boil nettles in the summer, and give hounds nettle soup. It is vital that hounds should be tough and have stamina. Young hounds that will not thrive, partly because they do not really eat, have a real disadvantage.

At this stage, all opportunities are taken for walking the youngsters out with the pack on exercise. This, over the months until summer, is invaluable. Young hounds learn from their huntsman and whippers-in to some extent, but they assimilate even more from the example of older hounds.

Sometimes in kennels one will see junior staff leading young hounds about on collar-and-chain or string, something they have not learned at walk. Then they must be trained to go in couples. I have known huntsmen who said they had never put couples on a young hound. That may have been so, but if something goes wrong – say, a batch of uncoupled young hounds bolts – then much good work and training is thrown away in a few minutes.

For young hounds that are difficult at first I am a great believer in using couples. Formerly they were first coupled with old hounds and then to each other. I think the use of couples is very much reduced now, but I cannot emphasise enough to young Masters, more particularly young Hunt staff, not to take risks. If hounds get away there can be real trouble, and not easily mended.

There is little more to be done with them until the hunting season is over. The older hounds have a let-down period and Hunt staff can then concentrate on the young ones. This brings the further thrill of seeing what has come home in terms of quality. I never look at young hounds until mid-February. Then if we have not had a frost for a day or two it is great fun to have them out. Masters and huntsmen can then get an idea of them.

But one of the charms of creating a new pack is that each of these newcomers is altering, literally every week, until next autumn. One that you thought in March looked pretty middling, by July may be a swan, and the other way around. Discovering it for oneself is all about hound psychology. Many young hounds only reveal their potential when they have shed their puppy coats, a process which can be slow. Mrs Gingell of the Cambridgeshire Harriers, a lady of great skill, says she can tell which hounds will be good at about 8–12 weeks. I do not have that art.

The walkers' comments on their puppies can be useful, particularly if a draft of young hounds is being considered before the hunting starts, but their way of going is likely to change, and there is more to it than that.

Foxhounds must behave as a pack, and although some obviously become brilliant, and others pretty good as individuals, it is as a unit that they are judged out hunting. A young hound that becomes too sharp in its first season, and then swollen-headed, is dangerous. When I first started hunting I congratulated a young hound on catching an old fox on its own. I was pleased, and I told it so. It was never any good again. It became too sharp, and beyond reformation.

In May the young hounds begin to be taught the ways of the world. In particular, we have to tell them what they must not do. I believe that modern educationalists say that you must stress the positive – tell the young what they are to do. I am not sure that this always turns out to be a particularly perceptive way of teaching hounds.

A major lesson to be learned is that they are not to chase dogs, cats, horses and particularly in many countries, sheep. Huntsmen and kennel-huntsmen have to be dog psychologists. Some young hounds can be put right by a reproof. It is well worth remembering that scolding one, catching its eye and fixing your own eyes to it, can be as deterring as a walloping. But if there is a genuine attempt to do something dangerous, such as assault a cat or sheep, then there comes a time when that hound must have a salutary lesson. Some of them can be hard-headed.

Hound exercise is used partly to get hounds fit – but much more importantly, to teach them the ways of the countryside, how to find their way home from far-flung places, and civility. It is invaluable to ride about the country, not against the clock, and to be able to stop and talk to people on the roadside, visiting farms without a young hound getting into the dairy and drinking all the milk, and generally instructing the youngsters in how to be a credit to the pack, wherever, and at all times.

Occasionally I have known a hound to be lost. In these days of travelling to meets in hound lorries, hounds cannot always find their way home and will instead go back to where they were unvanned. Then a hound may be out for a few days, which is worrying. A hound that has gone a bit wild is not easy to catch. Some kennel-huntsmen I have known are marvellous at it, and sometimes a puppy-walker can be called in to help. An Eton Beagles bitch which we had lost one September near Evesham, found us again when we were hunting there after the Christmas holidays, fat as butter. She was called Peaceful, and she turned out to be deaf.

Eventually, they will all be trained and will know their way around. No need to shout and scream at them. If you turn left, they turn left. That is all done by confidence, a certain amount of talking straight to them, and a good deal by jollying them along and keeping them happy.

Some people, perhaps because they are short-handed, use hound exercise merely as a method of clearing their wind, muscling-up and hardening their feet. Much enjoyment for man and hound is lost by that. When the first morning's hunting comes, then hounds should have had the benefit of everything which has been described. Then comes the moment when they are told very clearly what they must do – which is to hunt a fox, and nothing else.

# CHAPTER 4

# AUTUMN HUNTING

Of course it was not called 'autumn hunting' for most of Ronnie Wallace's hunting life, writes Michael Clayton. The beginning of the season was traditionally known as cubhunting, but the term 'autumn hunting' was introduced towards the end of the twentieth century to counter accusations by the anti-hunting fanatics that in the autumn hounds were hunting totally immature cubs.

The truth is that foxes born in the early spring of the same year are fully grown by the autumn and are far from little furry cubs so often seen gambolling in television wild life programmes.

Relying on the general public's very limited knowledge of hunting was part of the propaganda battle against the sport.

The importance of 'entering' the young hounds introduced into the pack that summer cannot be exaggerated. Mistakes and bad technique during cubhunting can affect a pack's hunting abilities crucially throughout the rest of the season.

Young hounds learn naturally a vast amount of hunting technique from their elders in the pack. It is the huntsman's responsibility to see that the whole pack is well versed in 'good practice', and his influence during cubhunting must be decisive but tactful.

Those of us who had the privilege of hunting with Ronnie Wallace in the Heythrop country and on Exmoor know that he adapted his technique to suit the widely different terrains. Coverts were sometimes 'held up' by the field when it was necessary to prevent hounds running into areas unsuitable for hunting at that time of the year, perhaps where there were standing crops or stock still grazing.

Early into the cubhunting season hounds were soon hunting with flow, running into the open between coverts now and again. He equipped his staff with whistles and only these were to be used as a means of communication with the huntsman.

Despite variations in technique, his basic principles in handling hounds remained the same, allowing them as much freedom as possible to use their intelligence and 'fox sense', whilst still obedient to the huntsman's voice and horn when appropriate. As long ago as 1962, when he was a decade into his great Heythrop Mastership, *Baily's Hunting Directory* published an article entitled 'The Genius of Ronnie Wallace'. It referred to his remarkable control over hounds:

> He does not make a fuss of them, nor does he raise his voice much, but when he wants them they fly to him, and appear to have an eye on his movements all day. Hounds like firmness, hate being shouted and nagged at, and appreciate the worth of the man who helps far quicker than do his two-legged assessors.
>
> Ronnie Wallace makes his hounds hunt themselves – there are no short cuts in their education. On a moderate scenting day the pattern is frequently as follows: in the morning a fox, well found, is hunted steadily for an hour or more until they catch him, with the huntsman active only at the start when he is occupied in getting them away together and seeing that they have plenty of room to settle. Thereafter he acts as an observer, giving them the minimum of assistance. There is something analogous to the tutorial system of teaching at Oxford or Cambridge during this phase.
>
> In the afternoon, with an improving scent, he casts aside, as it were, his cap and gown and steps in to help them rattle their fox and kill him in a brilliant burst of forty minutes across the Gawcomb Vale.

Wallace's cubhunting mornings were somewhat like the morning hunting in the season proper, described above, although he would put no pressure on hounds to produce a longer hunt. At the Heythrop I was surprised to see him allow the mounted field to place itself quite close to hounds when following them in the open, as well as lining some coverts.

'They need to get used to horses and the general heroosh of the hunting field just as much as the actual hunting of the fox,' he told me. Some modern huntsmen would be surprised just how close to hounds Wallace would sometimes allow his large mounted field to ride in the more enclosed country of the Cotswolds, although there was never any question of hounds being in any way interfered with by the horses. One of his second whippers-in in the 1960s was Hugh Robards who was to forge a reputation as a superb huntsman of the Co. Limerick, and nowadays hunts the Rolling Rock Hunt in Pennsylvania, USA.

He recalls that Wallace started hound exercise on the horses in June and he engaged in the unusual practice of letting on the whole pack at once. He did not like his hounds whipped, or even the thong hanging loose, said Robards.

'It ran through our minds that they should be corrected, but how? We did not have to wait long to see. The Captain got off his horse, walked into the pack and, looking them straight in the eye, he growled at them. He did not raise his voice, he kept it low, but the hounds knew they had done wrong.'

In contrast, although he always had a large entry, Wallace would at first only take out a few young hounds each morning cubhunting, introducing more to the pack as they entered.

The day before the first cubhunting fixture, Wallace met his kennel huntsman and first whipper-in Bill Lander, and Hugh Robards, and told them what he expected of them, and how

Cubhunting on Exmoor: R.E.W. and the Exmoor bitch pack in September, 1979, after meeting at Picked Stones Farm Gate.

cubhunting was to be conducted. They were to meet at 6 am and cubhunting would take place five days a week.

'He demonstrated on the hunting horn the call for when he wanted Bill and the call for when he wanted me,' Robards remembers, adding wryly: 'I don't know why he bothered with a call for me, as he never used it in the three years I was there . . . Cubhunting was conducted with the minimum of noise, no whip-cracking, no shouting at foxes, no galloping about, no jumping, just a tally-ho back if a fox was turned, or one short blast on the whistle if a fox went away . . . Cubhunting was a well organized affair with (the terrierman) Charles Parker's great knowledge of how many litters of cubs were to be found in each area, for the Captain was not about to wipe out the fox population. In some areas he would go to great lengths to cull as many as he could, and in others he would take a more liberal attitude, but on the whole the Heythrop country was very well foxed. It was nothing for us to arrive at the meet in the pitch dark and drop off Charles with his terriers on the way, so that he could stop an earth. How he found them in the dark I really don't know. Days were long, as we started as soon as it was light enough to see a couple of fields; we continued many days until midday or much later.'

During his Heythrop Mastership Wallace frequently took his hounds to Exmoor and Dartmoor in the spring, and I was among those who followed him there, and much enjoyed riding after hounds in such a spacious and beautiful environment.

When he took the Exmoor Mastership I was able to see him entering his hounds each autumn, using a markedly different technique to that he had displayed at the Heythrop. Hundreds of hunting people from all over Britain, and abroad, would visit Exmoor in the autumn to stand for hours in the early mornings watching Wallace hunting hounds. The moorland is one large covert, and on the broad Exmoor slopes his hounds could be seen drawing, finding and hunting their fox as if on an instructional blackboard. Wallace rejoiced in the freedom he could give his hounds on Exmoor, but his control there was perhaps even more remarkable. I have seen him stand on a hill top and cast them far across a valley to another hill where they spoke on the line of a fox which had been seen going away. The accuracy of his cast, and his control of his hounds at such a distance was amazing. He was a 'quiet huntsman', and always used his horn sparingly. He said that in his latter years he could not blow the horn at its full volume anyway, because his lips had become bruised by so many years of sharp contact with the mouth of the horn whilst riding in the hunting field. After hunting we would discus the morning over a hearty breakfast at Mounsey. I recall him enthusiastically describing his hounds' display of 'winding' their fox: catching the scent of the fox on the wind above the heather, and suddenly surging across the moor with a great cry and their heads up for a while, until they checked and then recovered the line with their heads down on the line of scent, accurately hunting their fox for several miles until they caught him in the open.

Wallace was always insistent that a hunt must have a 'beginning, a middle and an end'. He abhorred what he called 'mystery tours', and he always said that a huntsman who did not expect anything more than 'local hunting' would seldom achieve more than that. On Exmoor it was easier to see his skill in casting hounds accurately, and his patience in regaining a line apparently lost, so that his hounds acquired and retained the confidence to finish a hunt, either by catching the fox or marking it to ground.

He was particularly scornful of a growing habit in hunting publications of hunt reports recording points of three miles or even less.

'If you haven't achieved a point of four miles or more you haven't even left the parish,' he would say, urging me to use the blue pencil on reports of 'three mile points' submitted to *Horse & Hound*.

In an interview given while he was at the Heythrop with that great devotee of hounds, Daphne Moore, Wallace made the following observations on hunting hounds on Exmoor:

> It is marvellous because it is quite a different sort of hunting, and I think it's very interesting for us, and probably for people down there, to see the way the hounds hunt. They are used to hunting very *accurately* in this part of the world and they apply the same technique down there, which is very often different from the local packs, especially the moorland packs, and I think that both are very successful.
>
> Probably the disadvantage of our hounds when they get down there is that they don't quest so wide. I haven't always agreed with the local experts on how wide it's a good thing to quest. If you are drawing a lot of wooded hillsides, in Wales for instance, with none too many foxes, then hounds *have* to draw very wide; but I'm never too sure on the moorland, because always, or nearly always, they begin to indicate when there's been a fox about, and I've found at

different times if you 'poke about' and change direction a little bit, you nearly always find the fox. Finding the fox is, of course, a great art down there.

Dartmoor is an amazing place; very tough going, and hounds run faster than they do on Exmoor; you've an awful job to live with them. Foxes have strongholds down there, very often miles away, and they'll go straight for them with confidence. Quite good points at times.

He told Daphne Moore that when he first took the Cotswold hounds, prior to his Heythrop Mastership, he found that they had accounted for very few foxes the previous season.

'One of the interesting things that first summer when we arrived, was that you could go anywhere and see foxes walking about all over the place in broad daylight.

'That persisted until we started cubhunting, and I've often quoted it as an example of the way that hunting helps to control foxes. It's not entirely the number that are killed, but the fact that if they walk about as if they own the place, then they do damage because they are about in daylight and so on. If you bustle them about, split up the litters, then they return to their normal habits. That was noticeable, of course in many countries in the season curtailed by foot-and-mouth in 1968. It was an extraordinary sight: anywhere you went in the country where there were foxes, you could see them walking about everywhere, and then that stopped.'

Although 'autumn hunting' or cubhunting is traditionally entirely the Master's prerogative when providing sport for the followers is not the priority, Ronnie Wallace's skills were such that each cubhunting morning was a memorable example of a huntsman's mastery of the science of venery.

In the years at the Cotswolds and on Exmoor many will remember cubhunting with the Captain just as vividly as the season proper from the start of November.

CHAPTER 5

# THE HUNTSMAN'S
# TECHNIQUE – IN BRITAIN
# AND THE UNITED STATES

Ronnie Wallace was often at his best in describing his
version of the science, or art, of venery when discussing
it with other experienced huntsmen. He became especially
interested in hound breeding and hunting in the United
States, after being invited to judge hounds. His close friendship with C. Martin Wood III and his wife Daphne Wood
who founded their own Live Oak pack of foxhounds so
successfully in northern Florida, further increased his
involvement in US hunting, and he made many friendships
among American Masters.

On 26 January, 1990 Ronnie Wallace took part in a panel
discussion held in New York City following the annual
meeting of the Masters of Foxhounds Association of
America.

His fellow panellist was one of the great personalities of
US foxhunting, Ben Hardaway III who has created a legend
as a Master, amateur huntsman and innovative hound
breeder in his own Midland pack, hunting in Georgia and
Alabama.

Richard D. Webb MFH (Moore County Hounds) introduced the panel, and the moderator was 'Marty' Wood, a
former President of the American MFHA, a role currently
filled by Mrs Wood.

The discussion was lively and entertaining, giving
valuable insights into hunting the fox in the United Kingdom
and the US, plus some fascinating comparisons with coyote
hunting which has since become more widespread on the
Eastern seaboard of America, having spread from
the western states.

*Mr Webb:* Welcome to the panel. We're very honored to have our new honorary member, Captain Ronnie Wallace, Chairman of the MFHA, Great Britain, and our own legendary Ben Hardaway as a panel on fox hunting. The moderator this morning is your new president, Marty Wood. He and his wife, Daphne, are Joint Masters of the Live Oak Hounds in Thomasville, Georgia. Marty actively hunts his own hounds, a cross-bred and English pack. He hunts fox and coyote and, occasionally, bobcats. And I'm telling you, I've hunted with him and he is virtually a part of his pack. He is a hound himself in my opinion and your Association is in good hands. And without further ado, I'll turn the chair over to Marty to moderate the panel and please, as the panel progresses, think of questions that you might have and don't hesitate to ask them. Remember, this is a learning experience. If you're a new Master, don't be embarrassed to ask. We're all here to help. Thank you very much.

*Mr Wood:* Dick, before you step down, if you would, ladies and gentlemen: I waited until this moment because I wanted more people in the room other than just the members of the Association to say thank you to our retiring president. He has served this Association magnificently for the last three years. Those of you that have not had the pleasure of working with Dick Webb, do not know what a hard working, unstintingly devoted person he is to fox hunting. He literally lives, eats and breathes the sport. He's a great asset to our sport. He obviously is not leaving the board entirely. He will, of course, stay on as a director at large for a number of years. And Dick, on behalf of the entire Association, I'd just like to say thanks for a job very well done.

*Mr Webb:* Thank you. Thank you very much.

*Mr Wood:* You know, it's a very interesting thing for me to stand here with a paltry twenty years of experience in this business, between two living legends, that I would characterize as certainly the two greatest living amateur huntsmen of this century. Both of them are known for the cracking good sport that they provide with their hounds. Both of them are renowned hound breeders. Ronnie, of course, in Great Britain, Ben, here in the United States. They are annually the ones who sweep the boards at the major hound shows. But getting beyond the breeding and showing of fox hounds, we have an opportunity before us this morning to delve into over a hundred years of experience of hunting fox hounds. When I go down the list, and I just made a quick one, we have experience up here today with otter hounds, beagles, harriers, fox hounds, deer hounds, blood hounds, possum hounds, coon hounds, pointers, retrievers, basically all different types of sporting dogs. More importantly, these two gentlemen are great personal friends of mine. It gives me great pride to stand here and act as a moderator on this panel to the two men that have really been my mentors in my development in this sport. The format we're going to use this morning is one of question and answer. We hope to promote questions from the floor on the subject of fox hounds and fox hunting. This is your opportunity to ask whatever you'd like, within certain limits, of the two greatest living amateur huntsmen of this century. So, without further ado, I'll ask Ronnie to respond first, in deference to his high office as Chairman of the British Masters of Foxhounds Association and our new honorary member. I would like to ask, 'What is it that you look for in a fox hound to produce the type of sport that you provide in your country on the Exmoor?'

*Captain Wallace:* Mr Chairman, I think it's fundamental what qualities a hound needs, and I would put above all others a burning desire to go hunting and toughness. I think those are the two most important things. There are all kinds of qualities a hound needs because it's the only animal in the world that has to sprint and stay. So, you'll need nose, tongue, stamina, and you'll need drive, and, very important, a desire to conform with the huntsman and, of course, fox sense as well. If you are interested in conformation, and I believe you should be, then I submit that quality is the ingredient which is most dangerous to a fox, but there is one provision which is essential. If you have a very good looking hound, once it has reached its maturity and is entered, that hound if it wins a substantial prize at a hound show, must be better than the pack hound and if it isn't better than the pack hound for goodness sake get rid of it, because people will come and follow the fashion, use that hound and then you will get slack ones, and that goes against my first provision for the hound which is its desire to hunt.

*Mr Hardaway:* Right. In our country here and in my country, the first thing that I think about is: can I break that hound off deer and can I get him to do what I want him to do? In England, you can get at your hounds better, so the first thing that I look for in a hound is biddability. If I have a hound that's really hard-headed, even though he may have made a good hound later in his life, if he was terribly hard to break and he wouldn't break off deer, then I wouldn't use him. So my first quality would be biddability, a desire to please the huntsman and then after that I would go along with the rest of the qualities but if you can't break him, I don't care how good he is or how good looking he is or how good a nose he's got he's not much use to you.

*Mr Wood:* What would you expect from your huntsman? Both of these men have their own packs, but what are the essential qualities for a huntsman to have? We've talked about a fox hound now what do you think that other ingredient is? Mr Hardaway would you like to try that one first?

*Mr Hardaway:* What do you want in a huntsman? Well, as I must say, we are all looking for good people, and I fortunately have the best people. I've talked to quite a few people up here at this meeting, and I've decided the first thing to look for is a decent human being. I decided that there's no use going out and trying to find the greatest huntsman if he's a low down S.O.B. because you're not going to fool with him. So I tell people let's try to find the first quality that we want. It's like that hound, if he won't do what you want him to do he may be a demon, but he might as well be off in Arizona somewhere. So I say let's look for a decent person that you wouldn't mind sitting down and having a drink with, and having a nice conversation with, and then go from there, because there's so many people that can do the job floating around, but they're just not decent human beings and that's the first thing I look for in a huntsman, is a decent fellow, a decent human being. Same for a whip or stable person or anybody like that.

*Mr Wood:* Thank you sir. I believe you qualify on all those counts. Ronnie.

*Captain Wallace:* Yes, well he's got to be pretty tough, like the hounds, he's got to be quite brave, he's got to be desperately fond of hunting and in good health. But of course, if you're going to be a huntsman you've got to have that affinity with dogs which is undefined and if you have, it's the invisible string which is very fragile with some, a bit like parcel string with some others, and with a very, very few, as thick as a rope. If you have that ability to interest dogs, you can be a huntsman. If you haven't, you should try some other profession.

*Mr Wood:* Well said. Do we have some questions from the audience?

*Question:* I have one additional thing. I have to do a little background first. I've watched huntsmen who can walk hounds out, and walk them out every day and the hounds love them and those same huntsmen, in some cases, will cast their hounds in the covert and it doesn't seem like the hounds hunt for them. I've watched other huntsmen who hardly ever walk their hounds out or don't walk them out regularly, they have other people do it, and yet they can get on a horse to hunt their hounds and these hounds trust them from the moment they go in and they hunt for them. My question is how do you get your hounds to trust you?

*Mr Hardaway:* Well, I think first you have to trust them. I feel so many huntsmen put the wrong emphasis on what they want their hounds to do. I think I'm criticized at times when I take my hounds away from Midland if they all don't get right behind my horse, you know, and sneak along like this and, oh, they are scared to go here and scared to go there. They're flowing in and out but they're not going anywhere and I trust them that they're not going anywhere. It's like they say the tighter you pull the spring, the further it flies when you turn it loose. And if you keep those hounds all bottled up, if they're worth their salt, you know, if they have that nervous energy that makes them great hounds, and you keep them all tied up, there, well, he'll walk out great for you but he'll say wait until that S.O.B. turns his back buddy, I'm going to have my fun. But if you let him flow in and out, he feels comfortable with you and he's not going anywhere and you trust him, then when he goes to hunting he's going to trust you and he'll go hunting for you. But he's not going to go off and leave you. Does that answer your question?

*Audience:* Yes, sir.

*Mr Hardaway:* Well I guess it goes back to what Ronnie says, it's that invisible string, a feeling that you have with hounds and I guess some people have it and some people don't.

*Mr Wood:* Ronnie would you like to answer?

*Captain Wallace:* I think that is right. You see, you've got to do it in the summer, and I'm one of the people who've never, or haven't for nearly forty years, walked hounds out. An amateur huntsman is privileged to employ a top class first whipper-in and kennel huntsman and when you've got one of them, don't keep the dog and try to bark yourself. Early in the war, I had my beagles at the Royal Military Academy at Sandhurst. The old huntsman of the beagles there, a kennel huntsman who had been second whipper-in to the Duke of Beaufort, was a great fellow and he used to watch us cadets in the morning looking after the beagles.

'Very amateurish,' he'd say. And of course, that's what we

were, but it's the hunting in the field and this is done in the summer. Getting the hounds out, don't make any mistakes with them; with young hounds keep them on the couples until you're an experienced person. Don't let them get away from you. And then they get their confidence. When they get their confidence in you, you go exercise, and they go up the road and they get to the cross roads and the young ones say we went this way yesterday and, even if that's the way you were going, you'll go another way, and then they come along, and the old hounds'll scold them then, and they feel stupid you see. When you've got them like that, and they're standing there waiting – which way are we going this morning boss? – then you've got them. That's the basis. It's no good going hunting unless you've got the hounds. Some of us were soldiers once, and we were made to march about, and do what we were told. Didn't do us much harm and it's just like when we were at school. And it's just the same with the hounds. Be very firm with them, be very nice to them, get their confidence, and then you'll catch all the foxes in Christendom.

*Mr Wood:* Another question.

*Question:* I'd like to ask: how important is it for hounds to kill a fox? I know in England that's what they're supposed to do. In this country we'd maybe rather put them to ground so they could live to run another day. How many foxes have you killed . . .

*Captain Wallace:* In my life?

*Audience:* In your life.

*Captain Wallace:* I don't know. We kill a good many every year, but we have to, you see, it's part of the thing. We think it's very important to catch foxes. But I'm sure if you run them to ground and if you make some excitement for the hounds, marking that sort of thing, I dare say to some extent that does the same thing. Certainly hounds will still hunt even if you don't catch foxes. But I suspect they just haven't got that little bit of needle. You see, we think fox hunting is a hoorooshing sport. It's lovely to see the hounds hunt. It's lovely to hear the fellow say 'Oh they hunted all day and the huntsman never went near them.'

Well, if he didn't go near them, he's had the influence on them to make them hunt all day and, it's a quick sport. It's nice to see hounds work it out but at some point they've got to press the fox.

The joy of hunting is the combination of the hounds doing it and the huntsman too. Of course, when we get closer to fox, particularly when I used to hunt in the Midlands, look out there.

The man who taught me more about hunting than anybody was called Will Freeman and he was a very famous man. When I was a boy we used to go in the big woods at Eridge and Sussex, and he put the hounds in very early in the morning, and they'd run with a tremendous cry and divide into several lots. He'd ride about, and perhaps talk to the people he liked, which wasn't everybody. And then all of a sudden he'd see the fox cross the ride.

'We'll have him now!' he said, 'We'll have him now!' Then he'd get the hounds together; out would come his horn, whippers-in would be everywhere and they'd kill him handsomely. And those hounds were made. That's the secret of it.

*Mr Wood:* Ben would you like to comment?

*Mr Hardaway:* Well, I've never seen a hound that didn't seem to enjoy catching a fox. But I don't think that it's necessary to catch a lot of foxes to have a good pack of fox hounds. It's bred in them to run, and I think you can get good sport without catching a lot of foxes. It certainly, I would agree, does seem to add a little bit of zip in them, and it gives them that added desire, and so forth, when it gets to be a long run. And I've noticed in the new experience of running and occasionally accounting for a coyote, that after they account for a couple coyotes, they are a different, uh, machines. And it's no question to me that it certainly changed the attitude about that particular deal, so I think it's a factor, but I don't think it's an absolutely necessary factor.

*Mr Wood:* Before we take another question, perhaps we could embellish on something that Ronnie said, and that is the handling of a sinking fox. You heard him speak of Will Freeman and the way he'd do it. A sinking fox can be a difficult animal for a huntsman to handle. Ronnie, can you elaborate on that just a little bit?

*Captain Wallace:* Yes. To answer a lot of people in this room who don't want to catch foxes when the fox is, as you say, sinking, well then let him by, and either let him get to ground or let it peter out. For those who do want to catch the fox, this is a vital moment because, if you take them off their noses when you don't know where he is, you'll lose him.

I remember Hugh Robards, whom many of you hunted with in Ireland. Once, on a very windy day, we had a terrifically good hunt, and we ran into a field of brussel sprouts which in the autumn stink as well, and this fox was in the sprouts. Hugh Robards was second whipper-in, and he had his hat up like this, you see, and he just kept his hat pointed about two rows in these sprouts too long. I've got the hounds, I was there you see.

'Tally ho, look out, look out. Where is he, where is he, where is he?' and the beggar had laid down, and gone back behind us – and he ran and we lost him. I can remember it; I still wake up in the night and think how we missed that fox, you see? Good staff work, and you've got him, and the quicker you catch the fox of course when he's beat, the better for all concerned. So it is a combination of the hounds and the staff. Good staff are marvellous, but they must never put you wrong because if they once put you wrong you never forget it.

*Mr Wood:* Ben.

*Mr Hardaway:* We don't have as many occasions to handle a sinking fox in this country but, often times, if I feel my hounds are going to catch a fox, I don't like to stop my hounds abruptly from running a fox, because I don't think it does a lot of good. But I don't mind tricking them into losing him. I think you can do it without really having them lose confidence in you because, and I don't know whether Ronnie would agree, I think a fox's scent is a little less maybe when he's sinking and it's really difficult. The hounds really don't know whether I tricked them out of the fox or whether they really just lost him. And I do that quite often, particularly in the fall, with cubs and so forth. I'll trick them off and go on and draw somewhere else. But I do think it's a mistake to get your whippers-in abruptly and forcefully to stop your hounds when they've really run a fox good and hard.

*Captain Wallace:* We have to stop them, and I'm sure you do it, at dark sometimes and then it's quite a good practice to get off and talk to them, because hounds love you if you get off your horse. If your clothes are clean up until then, they won't be after that, but it's a grand thing. Of course, if you have hounds doing wrong, you've got to hit them sometimes but for goodness sakes hit the right one because if they beat you, they think they've got you. If you get off your horse and point your whip, and speak to them, and get a fix on their eyes, that can be as punishing to a hound as can anything really, but, be nice to them. I think hounds that are in form, don't mind being taken off the line sometimes as long as you don't do it all the time. They'll think you're a mug then, you see. If somebody hollers and you lift the hounds, I'm a great believer if you think it's the right fox. I'm a great believer in people hollering, I like hollering because people like hollering.

It's lovely to see a fox, but it's no good telling the fellow the next day: 'Oh, I saw your fox.'

It's too late then. I expect you'll get a good cussing sometimes. But then somebody hollers and I say 'shut up, shut up'. I know it, you see. But another day I shan't know then I say, 'Why the bloody hell did you tell me so late?' It was a busy fox hunt, you see; it's never the same twice. That's the lovely thing about it, you see. And you tell a fellow, you tell these whippers-in, I have to train these young whippers-in, I'm sure a lot of you do, I say, 'you bloody fools, you've done this and done that', and then the next time, of course, they do what you tell them, and it's wrong again because it's different.

(LAUGHTER)

*Mr Wood:* Ben.

*Mr Hardaway:* I was just going to wonder if that makes your whippers-in feel any better?

*Question:* I'd like to ask about something Mr Hardaway said that I didn't quite understand. How do you feel the hunting and killing of coyote affects the hounds when they hunt for us? I didn't quite understand what you mean, you said it made them a different machine when they hunt.

*Mr Hardaway:* Well, when the coyote first came in, my hounds seemed to look at it like coursing a dog. They seemed to be confused. I think the thing smelled pretty good to them, like something they ought to run, but when they ran up there and looked at it, they said, 'gee does that thing smell like that and look like this?' I've seen them run up to him and look at him and back off and trot over to me. Just like, you know, 'I'm sorry boss I didn't mean to course that dog.' They wouldn't run him by looking at him but when he got out of sight, you could lay them back on the scent and they'd go like a pistol. After they finally lucked into dispatching one or two, they didn't run up there and look at him any more. They are a different machine. Now, as far as it affects the hounds running a fox, I think they run the fox just as well, and a bobcat just as well, but I do think running a coyote tends to make them a little wild. Would you agree with that?

*Mr Wood:* I definitely agree with that.

*Mr Hardaway:* It makes them a little wild and if they are ever going to act bad on something it would be during a coyote race rather than a fox race, because I think the coyote smell [is stronger]. You can run a coyote on a day when you can not run a fox. I've run a fox up until ten o'clock in the morning and lost him. Then turn to

63

some visitor that I was trying to show a good time, and say, 'well, now I'll give you a run' and go out there and kick a coyote up and run him until one o'clock. He must stink, you know. He's bound to really be a strong smelling thing and I do think that strong smell gets them so excited and all that. If they're going to act bad, they're going to act bad on a coyote rather than a fox.

*Mr Wood:* The problem that we've seen, and if I could just embellish on that for a minute, is that when we run coyotes four or five times in a row, we have a hard time because they do smell so strongly and they're easy for the hounds to run. I have a had time getting my hounds back to where they really draw their coverts. What they want to do is go through the coverts rapidly and then, as Ben says, you know, it makes them a little bit wild and if there's any predilection to go off on a deer perhaps some of your young hounds might try it at that point in time. What I usually try and do is take the hounds to a grey fox covert where they've got to get in and root through a bunch of vines and briars to get them back on their noses and doing what they should be doing.

*Mr Hardaway:* I think it's asking a lot of a pack of hounds to run four different things. A grey fox obviously smells different than a red fox. I've had hounds that would run a red fox that wouldn't run a grey fox. Then you ask him to run a grey fox; you ask him to run a red fox, you ask him to run a bobcat and then you turn around, and ask him to run a coyote. And then you won't let him run a deer or a hare or a possum or a coon, although I've killed a few raccoons this year. But I think it's asking a lot of the mentality of a hound to run four things that obviously smell different to him, and then not run all the rest of the riot that's in the woods. Would you agree with that Ronnie?

*Captain Wallace:* I don't know much about it, but I should think it's better for them to run a coyote than to be drawing all day.

*Question:* We were talking about when a huntsman might get off his horse, and Marty was just talking about tougher animals and briars. What do you think is the best method when you get to a covert? Some hounds will go in, but not all of them are just going to dive in and root under there. What is the best method for the huntsman to get them into covert?

*Captain Wallace:* You've got to be very patient. I've seen people try to drive them in, but that's not a bit of good. The hounds do it by smoozing really if the fox is about, they'll go in, and you can draw through a lot of big woods and they don't seem to be taking much interest and then all of a sudden they disappear and then they're fine. And the worst thing is all the pheasants that the people grow nowadays. They foil the ride, what we call the rides; trails, I think you call them, in the woods, and hounds can't smooze. You can, by all means, go in on foot, it's bad for the boots, but when I was younger I used to draw on foot a bit because you want to get hounds together, do you see? It's drawing, it's like a lot of other things to do with hounds. It's balance and hounds have got to spread out and draw, but you can get a hound that draws so wide that he finds a fox and you never get the other hounds to him, and then you spoiled your hunt. We get that on the moors because the foxes lay any old where and I used to see hounds when I went down there, particularly on Dartmoor, that would go tremendous distances and in a wind you never do get them together. I brought some hounds down there once because where we used to visit in the spring, at the Heythrop we put in an extra day or two, and the local pack lent me five couple. They found a fox, we never got near them and, so we might as well not have taken them to start with, because they went far; miles further than ours did.

*Question:* Given the difference in cry when hounds run deer, do you notice any difference in their tone between fox and coyote?

*Mr Hardaway:* Well I used to say I could tell when my hounds were running deer by the cry, but I was fooled a couple of times so I quit saying that. I'm not going to say really that I can tell the difference between a fox and a coyote because if you say that, and you're right a couple times, then you'll get on a fox that really screams away and you'll be wrong so I don't think I can. No.

*Captain Wallace:* I don't know. When you find a fox they're different to a deer because it's generally a sort of little bit of a muffled noise isn't it, a squeak in the briars and you're pretty sure that's right. Whereas if a hound goes away, yap, yap, yap, yap, yap it's likely to be wrong. But I don't know with a coyote. Do you find him in the thick or, or does he . . .

*Mr Hardaway:* Could be anywhere.

*Captain Wallace:* I mean that's generally the way of it isn't it, to tell the difference.

*Question:* This is a question really that I'd like to hear both gentlemen answer. How do you deploy your whippers-in, and where do you want them when hounds are running?

*Captain Wallace:* Well, I want one on each flank, and they want to be far enough forward to see the fox if he goes there, or he goes there, if possible to give you a signal. We use a whistle. We find that very useful, but by jove if they divide, and one lot go back, this fellow'd got to drop out of heaven and stop them quick and bring them on. Some people have their first whipper-in with them to open the gates and put hounds on if you want them out of the covert. They used to say professional huntsmen take their first whipper-in into covert with him; amateur huntsmen take a pretty girl. That's a very good arrangement if she's up to the job. But you don't want a fellow just about you all the time putting them on. We used to call that donkey walloping; dog walloping, do you see; or the use of the expression 'Get away hark'. I hate that; always cheer the hounds unless they're wrong, always cheer the hounds, the whippers-in cheer them on, cheer and that's how it should be.

*Mr Hardaway:* I've got two whippers-in and I've got one on the east side and one on the west side. They are out far enough and our country's pretty wooded in Georgia and pretty open in Fitzpatrick and I want one on each side and out far enough to where they can do me some good. And I usually have somebody in the field that can help. If I need somebody right now, I just turn to somebody nearest to me, hopefully a good looking girl, but sometimes anybody and I just say: 'Ya'll, would you stop those hounds for me?', or do this or do that, and I want my whippers-in to ride a pretty good ways out.

*Captain Wallace:* I think it's a dangerous thing, if I might suggest it. People who help you in the field are a wonderful thing, provided they do it when you ask them. But you don't want a lot of people shouting at the hounds, you know, because it upsets them.

*Mr Wood:* Ronnie, on Exmoor, you hunt big cleeves and steep coombes where, if a hound would go out the bottom and up the other side, it's almost impossible for you to be right with them. Ben's country, on the other hand, has got these big old river bottoms and swamps where hounds can go out the back side, and it would be impossible for the huntsman to get right to them. How do you feel about a whipper-in going on with hounds, if they come out that side and it's obvious that the fox has gone away?

*Captain Wallace:* We do it all the time. Mr Hardaway thinks I'm a lot older than him, but he hasn't done his sums too well. I have got pretty old, so I like my whippers-in to cheer the hounds, and go on with them, and I'll arrive sometime.

*Mr Hardaway:* Yeah, I think your whipper-in, if you throw them

66

R.E.W. and the Heythrop pack proving that hunting can be an all-weather sport.

out to him should go on. I used to throw them out. One time I was riding along with a strange person, and I said: 'That's a thrown-out dog', and he said: 'I sure heard a lot of breeds; what breed is that?'

If I'm thrown out, I expect my whipper-in to stay there. He's the head man until I get there, and he's got to go on; he's got to stay with the hounds, and he's got to use his initiative then to do what's necessary in whatever situation arises.

*Question:* The expression is that a fox well found is half killed. I'd like to hear Ben and Ronnie talk about that and specifically about taking hounds to a view without getting them overly excited.

*Captain Wallace:* Yes, I think we've talked about that already to some extent. If you get hounds finding very wide, you want to get them all off together if you possibly can. One of the criteria of a really good pack of hounds is their ability to catch up, to go away from a covert. In the part of the world I used to hunt in, we had thick coverts and you blow them away provided you've got their attention. Then they'll come and they'll get together if they're a good pack of hounds. If they're not a good pack of hounds, the Duke of Beaufort told me once: 'The difference between hounds when I was young and now', (this was fifteen years ago), 'is that they're much more together. They used to run in a much longer line in days gone by.' I can't remember what the other point you made about that was.

*Mr Wood:* Taking hounds to a viewing without getting them overly excited.

*Captain Wallace:* Yes, well now, this is very important. Because if you're going to a holloa, you've got to go, and it's no good fiddling about, because if you don't go, then the field will. Then you're done for. And so, when if you've got several foxes about, as I tell you I always took somebody with me that knew what to do. They needed to have the gate open when you got to the other side where they holloaed the fox away. But you must have somebody with you, then it's the one time you want to make plenty of noise if you're going to a holloa. If I am casting the hounds I never say a word. Some people say, 'yut, yut, yuy,' like that, you see, when they hit the line, but I don't do any of that; I just swing them, and then on the horn perhaps toot, toot, toot like that, and they keep coming around. But if you're going to a holloa, get there, and have the fellow waiting for you with his hat. There's some people gallop off the last place they saw the fox. You tell them to put the hat on, and come back to where they first saw him. Then point the hat. Mind the heel way because, there was a fellow once who said: 'That's no good; that's heel way. Well,' he said, 'he must have come from there', but he didn't catch many foxes that way.

*Mr Hardaway:* Well I'm glad to hear Ronnie say that, because I think when I was up in Virginia, I might have been criticized for holloaing and running to the viewed fox. But it's a great feeling to have a view, by golly, for a huntsman, that's a huntsman's dream. You've got a fox to run, you know it's a fox, you basically know which way he's going, if you can't run that one, you'd better turn in your suit. It's easier for me to keep my hounds from getting excited and acting crazy, than it is for myself. I mean I'm the one that gets excited and holloas and raves, but the hounds seem to be patient enough, and they put up with it. You finally get there, and it's a wonderful feeling to lay them on the line and see them go away.

*Captain Wallace:* We're talking about holloaing and the desirability of holloaing. It's so important for people to know what the huntsman wants to know what he comes to where you're holloaing. It is exactly where you last saw the fox, and you'll be where you first saw the fox so you've got some leeway to make up, which direction he was going in and how long ago. There was a fellow in our part of the world who said to Lord Knutsford when he was hunting Lord Bathurst's hounds in the VWH Hunt before the war, he was waving his hat like that you see, and his lordship said: 'Have you seen him?'

'No, no' he said, 'but he always goes this way. Now you hurry up.'

*Question:* Along those same lines, I've found, if I do holloa is that, particularly some of our older hounds will come right there, they don't wait for the huntsman. What do you do about that? The most desirable thing is to have the pack run together, but some of the clever ones come right to the holloa. They're gone and on line before the rest of the pack can get there sometimes.

*Mr Wood:* The question is: what do you do, if as a whipper-in, you are at the holloa, and some of the older more clever hounds come straight to the holloa instead of coming on with the huntsman? What should I do?

*Captain Wallace:* You must just steady them. Steady them till the others come. Or if the huntsman isn't far away, cheer them, what we were talking about before, you see. We'd come up out of these deep coombes, up over, as we say, and hounds would come on, and Tony Wright, if he's whipping-in for me, or the other whipper-in, they get on the brow. You must get where hounds can hear you. A lot of people get on the top, and think hounds can hear them. Well, the sounds go clean over them. Get where they can hear, and cheer them, cheer them you see, nothing like it.

*Mr Wood:* I'll say one thing on that same line, those of us that run coyotes, the worst thing that can happen to you, hunting a coyote, is to let two or three hounds get away, too quickly, because the rest of the hounds are going to spend the rest of the day hunting those other hounds, because they'll never catch up with them unless you're just plain lucky and have a check.

*Question:* I have a question and, that is, I read somewhere recently that in England the style is where the huntsmen hunt the fox helped by the hounds, whereas in America the style is where the hounds hunt fox helped by the huntsman. Is there really a distinction, and if there is, what is the proper balance between the hounds hunting their fox with a little assistance from the huntsman, or the huntsman really hunting the fox pulling his hounds along to help him?

*Captain Wallace:* There's room for both. You see, you mustn't be dependent. People always say, 'oh we haven't had sport, there hasn't been a scent.' It's no good waiting for a scent in this world to show sport, and your hounds should be able to show sport on any day except the odd hopeless one. You can have better runs on half a scent and a holding scent than you can on a very good scenting day. Foxes know it's a very good scenting day and they'll get to ground quick if they can and won't run so well. I once had a nine mile point, that's as the crow flies, and there wasn't any scent at all. I don't mind telling you now I take a few liberties but the hounds, it was late in the season and they enjoyed it, knew what we were doing just the same. We didn't catch him but he got to ground right down in the VWH country. We slotted him once, do you know what slotting is? That's a deer hunting expression. We tracked him in the cultivated ground.

*Mr Wood:* I always knew you had some Red Indian in you.

*Captain Wallace:* Ikey Bell you see, was a marvellous fellow to tell us all about hounds. You knew him, Ben, didn't you?

*Mr Hardaway:* Yeah, I met him.

*Captain Wallace:* Great man, but he'd try it on with you. He was talking to me one day and he'd come up to London especially to see me because he'd heard I was using a dog he didn't approve of. He said about another one, of course, he's a marvellous dog on the down in the spring. He said that he can bow wow all across the freshly cultivated ground. He was watching football but he looked at me to see whether I'd swallowed it. Because if I had, he wouldn't have had any more to do with me, I can say that.

*Mr Wood:* We're talking about the huntsman helping the hounds.

*Mr Hardaway:* I'm all for it. If you can help your hounds, and you don't, I think you're making a big mistake. I think it's a mistake when you try to do something when you don't really know what to do, you better leave them alone. As Ronnie said, there's room for both and if you really know what to do, and you really know what the situation is, I think you're making a big mistake not to handle your hounds properly and get them to do what you want them to do.

*Mr Wood:* Wouldn't you say that is part of what adds that invisible thread between the huntsman and his hounds, when you know what's right, and you can help your hounds and that just strengthens that cord?

*Captain Wallace:* You see, if you hear some people who go hunting with you, discussing the situation and they say: 'By jove, we did have a good day today, and as for that old huntsman, he might just as well have been at home in bed.' Now that's high praise. Because those hounds have been influenced in the right way.

*Mr Hardaway:* In certain parts of America I think the huntsman that does pick his hounds up and does go to a holloa, and does try to help his hounds get unjustly criticized for over handling his hounds. Well, you know, you have got thirty or forty people back there trying to have some fun. I know when I'm out there that's what I'm trying to do. I'm not going to hurt my hounds trying to show them fun, but by golly, we're out there to put on a performance. I think it's unjust to criticize. You know that everybody's always wanting to say let the hounds do it, let the hounds do it. Well that's all well and good if they can do it, but when they can't do it, then that's what I figure I'm getting paid to do.

*Captain Wallace:* You never want to be wasting a second on a hunting day. No stone left unturned to show sport. If hounds are fiddling it across some bare ground or something you can get hold of one or two reliable ones and be making the ground good beyond that. It is just as important for a huntsman to find out where the fox hasn't gone because when he's discovered that, it'll turn out where he has gone.

*Question:* My galloping fields are interspersed with huge coverts, and there are rides through them so that my field master can take the field and follow the pack when it's running. But my experience is that I can stay exactly where I am, and because I know the coverts, I know where they're likely to run, and then the pack'll run them and come back to me and off we go. How do you get them to break out of those huge coverts to give a little more of a straight out run, and keep them from just staying in the woods when you have big dense coverts?

*Captain Wallace:* One word. Pressure.

*Mr Hardaway:* I'd cross old Byron on a couple of your bitches and I believe that fox would come out of there. Ronnie said the word, pressure. If you've got hounds that are just booh-booh-ing about him, he'll stay there all day, but you go putting the heat on him, and I guarantee he's coming out of there.

*Captain Wallace:* He will break out. If you press a fox at the start,

71

and then he gets away from you, which they mostly will, you can hunt him out then with a good chance of finishing the hunt well. But if you start just desultory hunting, miles behind, you'll never do any good.

*Question:* If you're hunting a fox and somebody holloas, and it's obvious to you that it would be much quicker to take your hounds up and go to the holloa will you do that or won't you?

*Captain Wallace:* Yes, if it's quicker to get there. But it's up to you to decide, whether it's the right fox or not, and that's part of the huntsman's skills and if you're wrong, you're wrong. But you see, people say, like early in the season, 'oh they'll only run around in circles.' But there'll be good foxes making back for where they came from in the spring. And if you've got a good staff and they can give you a signal. That's the advantage of the whistle you see, and you can get the hounds and away to go.

*Question:* I'd like to ask Ben and Ronnie if a fox going away from cover has control over how much scent he's putting out. Many times we think that a scared fox does not give off much scent. Deer hunters I know think a scared deer, coon, possum everything else, gives out more scent.

*Captain Wallace:* I quite agree with you if I've got the point right. If you've got a thick place where you're hunting, and you see these cubs just walking about, just tiptoeing about I think you said your hounds can't have them, but if you can get at them, and get them bustled, they'll run entirely differently. Funny isn't it?

*Mr Hardaway:* But I also think, Ronnie, say you're running a fox and he comes up on somebody and is frightened or say a sheep dog runs him for the length of this room, doesn't that change it? Doesn't something happen there because when your hounds get there a lot of times you're in trouble for a ways.

*Captain Wallace:* I learned when I hunted the beagles as a boy, and you'd see an old hare come through the runners, through the fields you see. This old hare would go like that, and her ears would go back and forward. Those beagles hunted very well, but they couldn't hunt her until they got clear. Something to do with the glands. I suppose.

*Mr Hardaway:* I don't know what it is, but if you scare a fox, or I guess a hare, and you frighten it there for awhile, the hounds don't seem to be able to run it until it gets on out. Then I guess it settles down and goes back to relaxing or something. I don't think anybody knows exactly what it is, but I think that's a fact, that it's difficult, I think that's what you were saying isn't it?'

*Captain Wallace:* You may have seen the illustration 'Mr Jorrocks. Count twenty, let the Fox go', and then count twenty before you start holloaing him. Because otherwise it can turn him, or put him off the stroke.

*Mr Wood:* Particularly to let him get out of sight before you start all that holloaing.

*Question:* I wonder if Ben could expound a little on breaking of hounds off deer.

*Mr Hardaway:* Very, very quick. Sixty per cent of getting your hounds steady to deer is the way they're bred. I don't think you, per se, can breed a hound that will not run a deer but I think you can breed hounds that are so biddable and so tractable and want to please you to where a minimum amount of discipline will make them realize that's wrong. I break maybe sixty puppies a year, me and my staff, and I don't break anything but they break them. But if I took one of your hounds that's been running deer for ten years and his daddy ran deer for ten years, and I put that dog on my bitches, well me and my staff couldn't break but about ten hounds a year. You get the point I'm making? Sixty per cent of this whole job is to breed hounds properly. If you get hounds from Ronnie, and he's been hunting them over Exmoor for ten

Ronnie Wallace at Peterborough 2001 with Marty and Daphne Wood III, Joint Masters of their Live Oak pack in Florida, USA.

years he's not running the red deer, he's running through, he's running foxes through the red deer. I guarantee the hounds, whether Ronnie wants to give them to you or not. I guarantee you they are going to be easier to break off deer than hounds up in Leicestershire that haven't seen a deer in forty years. So the first thing to do is to get a strain of hounds that have been running deer country from somebody who has tried to breed so that you can break them off deer. Then you want to start them out as early as possible. There are all sort of tricks such as letting them smell a deer gland and shocking them and I think that's good but that has to be done between the ages of eight and eighteen weeks. Or you can put a little deer scent on a rat trap and let him smell it as a puppy and it'll snap his nose and all that helps. I keep a herd of goats around my kennels and they trot through goats from the time they're puppies and all that helps. And then you got to go out there and you got to walk them through deer every time you walk them out, you want to try to walk them through deer and you want to rate them when they run deer. Then by the time they're a year old, and you start hunting them, they're pretty well broke.

*Mr Wood:* I think a common error here is that people try to avoid deer. That's the opposite of what you should be doing. You should have them in deer all the time.

*Captain Wallace:* But it gets back to this business of trusting the hounds because I'm sure the foxes will do what they do in our country, which is run the same line as the deer. They're all stag hunters in our part of the world. All these old farmers, grand fellows, but, they'll tell you you're running deer and of course you eventually get to a hole or something and you say; 'Well, it's a funny looking stag's gone down there.'

*Question:* Some huntsmen with timid hounds in their first season will not rate them if they get off on deer, especially during a poor scenting day, simply because they want to encourage that hound on hunting. How do you feel about that?

*Captain Wallace:* Yes, I can see the point. I can see that could be the case. But Barber our hound, Exmoor Barber, not Orange County Barber, I saw him pursuing a deer one morning, and I wasn't hunting the hounds, as I don't hunt the dog hounds now. I said, 'Barber,' like that, you see, and he looked across the valley, 'Oh', he said, 'Is that the wrong thing to do?' and, 'Oh, I suppose it is.' And back he went you see. Nothing timid about him. I don't like timid hounds.

*Mr Hardaway:* Personally, I don't care whether he's timid or what he was, if he's running deer. I'm not going to let him run a deer. Now sometimes if my puppies jump a hare, I'm not gonna jump down their throat because I know they're only going to run him about as far as this room and then they are going to trot back to me, I mean I think it's just a mistake if they get after a hare. They are not going anywhere. But now a deer he's a different one. He's a different critter. I mean I don't want him to run. I don't want my hounds to run a deer one step. I mean when they smell that deer I want them to look back at me and come on back to me and be acquitted. That would be my feeling.

*Question:* You said that when you don't want to kill a fox that you can very often trick them off that line. What are the tricks that you use when you do that?

*Mr Hardaway:* Well, usually, as I said, the scent's probably fading a little bit and they're getting down on their noses and they make a little check. And I just sort of ease them along the wrong way, particularly if I saw the fox go a certain way. I just ease them along a different way and trick them away from where the fox is, or where I think the fox is, and you know, they'll think I'm casting them. I am, but I'm casting them in the wrong direction and that's what I mean by tricking them and then, like Ronnie said, then I get down and I pet them and I ask forgiveness for lying to them.

*Captain Wallace:* Is that the only time you ever have to ask for forgiveness?

*Mr Hardaway:* Well to my hounds.

*Question:* What sort of forgiveness do you have to ask in these days when you need to break them off highways, or railroad tracks or out of a new housing development? It seems that everyone of our countries has at least one side that has one of these obstacles that, viewed fox or not, it's time to stop.

*Mr Hardaway:* I know. We have it particularly with the coyote. You know, you get after a coyote and run him about forty minutes and he'd go right across Manchester Expressway and you've got to stop them and sometimes you have to shoot. They're so keyed up, you have to shoot your pistol to stop them and it's really confusing to them and it's hard on them and you hate to do it. But you can't do anything else. That's when I think you need to get them back and get down and let them jump on you and pet them and get their spirits back up and ask forgiveness. Isn't that about right Ronnie?

*Captain Wallace:* Yeah, we're with you.

*Mr Wood:* I use both of these gentlemen's hounds in my breeding program. Two weeks ago I had to stop hounds on a coyote. We had a blazing fast run. It was maybe fifteen minutes long. They were going straight at a shooting preserve that had 6,000 Mallard ducks on a pond. That was a lot of trouble. When I got to them I saw the coyote; he was forty yards in front of the hounds and we were seventy-five yards from the preserve boundary. It was simply a question of getting in front of them, getting their noses up, getting them off the line with as little fuss and bother as you can and then literally bale off that horse and tell them how much you love them. Because otherwise you do break their hearts. Going back to what Ben said about deer proofing, a lot of that is in the breeding. If you breed knot headed, hard headed hounds, that it takes a pistol to stop, then that's exactly what you're going to get. But if you've got biddable hounds that know and trust you then you can get away with it but you don't want to do it too often.

*Question:* On the question of showing good sport in the field, there's always a question of how you handle the situation when you're collecting your pack moving from one covert to another? How long do you feel it is reasonable to keep your field waiting while you're calling in hounds before you move on? I just sort of like you to continue on there.

*Mr Wood:* Ronnie, you want to take a shot at that?

*Captain Wallace:* Well, it all depends on how valuable your subscribers are. I think you can over do this waiting for hounds. The only trouble is if you get on the wrong side of some big road or railroad or something and you don't want to leave hounds there. Then you've got to hang on. Under normal circumstances you can wait too long for hounds because if you keep waiting for them, they'll keep you waiting.

*Mr Hardaway:* I agree. I travel all over the country. A lot of my meets are an hour away from kennels, and you know if I take a hound down to say, the Cedar Heights country about four times and it stays down there three times and we have to drive back and forth. Then I mean somebody else can ride up and down the road looking for that fellow and I get rid of it. Usually, when I get through hunting and blow my horn, within ten minutes all my hounds are sitting there looking at me. Obviously sometimes you are going to leave a hound out, or one's going to be slower. But if he's slow every time, you don't want that kind of fellow. I mean you don't want hounds you got to sit around all day waiting on.

76

*Captain Wallace:* Hounds dividing is the principal reason why you leave hounds out of the pack. In our country there can be quite good scenting on the right days, and if they divide, they can go for miles. You can get a hound that is a divider and he will just go wide and they've got heavy tongue and away he goes, and then keep dividing the pack. My dear old kennel huntsman said to me when I was hunting the Cotswold and he was hunting the Heythrop: 'If they get in the habit of dividing, you've got to stop it.'

R.E.W. announcing results at a Heythrop puppy show, with his kennel huntsman Bill Lander.

*Question:* We talked a lot about live hunting. I was wondering if you find if you drag sometimes or if you have a pack that's been used to a drag, if they have problems with live hunting again.

*Captain Wallace:* I think it might be very difficult, hounds that have been drag hunting, I wouldn't have thought they'd be great fox hunters after that.

*Question:* I'd like to address a question to both Ben and Ronnie. When you've finished hunting are you using a reward for the hounds who come in, and if so what are you using?

*Captain Wallace:* No, I hope we reward them with a fox at the end of the run. No, what do you think? Some bags of sweets?

*Audience:* I don't know, sir; that's the question.

*Captain Wallace:* That is very, very nice for the huntsman. If you please the huntsman, you see, then the hounds'll be pleased too.

*Mr Hardaway:* I do reward my hounds when I blow them in at the end of the day. I don't know whether it does them any good, it does me a lot of good. I'm a great chicken neck feeder and I keep a cooler of chicken necks in the hound truck.

*Captain Wallace:* Do you?

*Mr Hardaway:* And when I get my hounds together, while I'm throwing them chicken necks and petting them and generally associating with them, my huntsman is calling out their names and we check them off name by name. I hunt about sixty hounds and I can't count over thirty, so I have to check them off name by name. While that procedure's going on I throw them chicken necks, and they seem to appreciate it. I really think coming in, and being biddable, is more in the way they're bred than the chicken necks, but you know, I enjoy doing it so I'll keep on doing it.

*Mr Wood:* I think the difference here really is that on Exmoor Captain Wallace expects to kill foxes as differentiated with hunting here in the United States. Other questions, in the back there.

*Question:* When you're line breeding hounds, and you get a couple of strains that you really like, what are the clear indications that you've gotten too tight and need an outcross?

*Captain Wallace:* I suppose that you'll get weakness. I've never really seen that, and I think you can get very close with hound breeding, providing you know that what you're breeding into is the best. Certainly as far as these outcrosses are concerned, which I think are wonderful things, what you've got to do is to integrate them into your sort again as soon as possible. If you like your own type of hound and the female lines that are good plain cooks, they're the ones and you can do anything with them because you've not bred through the male. And it's a marvellous animal to breed because the turnover's so fast and you've got litters instead of just one foal or something like that. But if you get these outcrosses don't go too far out. Go out once and then bring it back to the sort again. But I should think if you get too closely bred, you'd get conformation problems and weakness.

*Mr Hardaway:* I've only recently really inbred one strain trying to get heavier cry and the litter seems to be doing pretty well. I'm not a great believer in really close inbreeding, although I read something the other day that the Seeing Eye dog people had bred these Labs for thirty years, and that they never bred a bitch over three years old, and they intensely inbred these seeing eye dogs, and that the best females came from a mother bred to her son, and the best males came from a father bred to his daughter. Those dogs have to be intelligent, and they have to have good physical qualities to lead the blind around, but I wouldn't try that myself.

*Captain Wallace:* A fox hound's got to do a great deal more than the animal you have described. There was a Colonel who owned a big estate in the Cotswold country when I first went there, and he had a private pack, from just about the first war until 1934. He had all sorts of theories, and he bred his hounds on the wolf system whereby he just let them breed. I believe they were very good hounds, but when he went to sell them at the hound sales they all had red mange, and I don't know whether that had anything to do with it or not.

*Mr Hardaway:* It probably did.

*Captain Wallace:* He was a splendid man. He didn't get on with the Master of the Cotswold who complained about the number of times his hounds had run from the peripheries of the country right into the middle of the Cotswold country. All he replied was: Please write on thinner paper!

*Mr Wood:* As a follow-up to that question I'd like our two panelists to address, how many lines do you attempt to keep in your kennels in levelling up a pack through your breeding program?

*Captain Wallace:* The more female lines you can have, the better. The whole secret in my view, of breeding hounds is the tail female, the solid base, and the tail male, and I'd rather look at the top line or the bottom line than anything else, and the more of those that you can keep, the wider your options. Some people have only got one female in the kennel, but I'd try and get one or two more if you could. I told Mr Hardaway that last night; he was listening too.

*Mr Hardaway:* I hope you'll follow up on that. I've got a good line that Ronnie's talking about, but it's through his dog hounds rather than through a bitch, and I hope that he'll not forget this, and send me that bitch we were discussing last night.

*Question:* We talked about whether or not the shape of a hound's head is going to influence its behaviour and attitude in the field. And this because there was some correspondence in *The Chronicle* last summer after the hound shows in which one man complained that the American hounds' heads have become so flat that they looked very English. And that he was hoping to get back to the more of the occipital bump because it was traditional. Now do you think that the shape of the head has anything to do with the way they work in the field?

*Mr Hardaway:* Well I think that certain physical and visual characteristics around the head go with certain invisible characteristics that go into the hound. Tom and Elsie Morgan, they wouldn't have a hound that had that occipital bump. They

American Masters: at a joint meet of the Belle Meade and Midland Hunts, l. to r.: Daphne Wood MFH (Live Oak), Dick Webb MFH (Moore County), Liz McKnight MFH (Elkridge Harford) and 'Duck' Martin MFH (Green Spring Valley).

wanted a hound's head flat and they said that all the hounds they ever had with those big bumps up here, and like that were too slow and too houndy to suit, to live with their pack. I do think that certain physical characteristics that you can visually see are linked with certain genetic characteristics that you want, or don't want, that you can't see. What would you say Ronnie?

*Captain Wallace:* I'm not too worried about the shape of the hound's head, but I can understand people over here who want to keep their sort. I think that's a very good thing to want to do, but the only thing that worries me about the hound's head is that its mouth is level because that can affect, obviously, its feeding and constitution. If you get swine chop and that's fairly hereditary. I don't know, we get quite a lot of these hounds with domed heads now with our Fell blood and our American blood and I haven't found any harm in it yet.

*Captain Wallace:* Hounds that are all the same sort are very attractive and probably run in the same style and pace.

*Mr Wood:* Ronnie wouldn't you say that it's a very important thing to have a level pack of hounds in the way they perform?

*Captain Wallace:* Yes I would, you know, on terms of catching foxes. I'd worry about a lot of other things before I'd worry about the shape of the hound's head. I'd far rather see its elbow and its loin, thank you very much.

*Question:* How much would you worry about size? Our best strike bitches have turned out to be somewhat undersized. Their male litter mates more normal size. They tend to be a little shorter which seems to work out fine in our country. It's fairly dense.

*Captain Wallace:* If they've got good bodies they'll breed bigger ones again. Practically, it's the ones that are small and weak, light of rib and that sort of thing and herring gutted. You're getting into dangerous country there, if you have one like that, but if you've got good bodies, little hounds, and you see, dog hounds used to be much bigger and I can remember the time when we used to think that the big one, the big dog hound, beat a good little one. Well you don't want too many small dog hounds. At Badminton, you see, they used to go in for very big dog hounds, but with these wire fences that nowadays, by jove, they have a job to get through don't they, especially dog hounds for some reason something to do with their anatomy. So I'd keep a good medium sized dog hound, twenty-four to twenty-five inches. And bitches, well they can be a bit smaller but, but don't keep breeding small ones generation after generation. You can get them back up again.

*Mr Hardaway:* I think you have to make an effort to breed bigger hounds. I think if you just let nature take its course it's what some breeders call the drag of the breed. It'll drag down to a mean; so I personally make an effort to breed bigger hounds, not because I think they're that much better, but just to try to keep a good level, what I call medium. In other words, my feeling to keep a good medium size pack of hounds, you've got to make an effort to breed bigger hounds or you'll end up with little ones. All of them little bitty hounds. That's sort of been my experience and I have a hard time keeping my bitches like what you're talking about. I have a hard time keeping my bitches up even, you know, medium size or bigger than medium size.

*Mr Wood:* Sherman, you had a question?

*Question:* If you have a hound who is honestly running usually way up in front of your pack most huntsmen or many huntsmen will cull that hound. What's your attitude?

*Captain Wallace:* He needs to be gone. Because he's there, he can't be there every time by fair means, and you'll spoil your pack. I did once have a bitch, big bitch too, that was too fast for our hounds and we had a marvellous hunt one October right into the Warwickshire country, and I'd just got to a road and saw her disappear out of the road a quarter mile in front and I galloped as hard as I could with the rest of the hounds, and put them on in the field. We killed the fox in another two fields but that bitch I'm sorry to have to tell you, went off hunting after that and I think she was too good for us, but you see she'll spoil your pack because it's dog hunting dog.

*Mr Hardaway:* I would agree with that and they are the hounds too that run way ahead and run wide that make you change a lot. You know I love a fast hound but, like Ronnie said, it's hard for a hound to be that far ahead every time if he's not cutting or cheating or getting up there by purpose.

*Mr Wood:* A hound like that'll soon break the hearts of the other hounds.

*Captain Wallace:* It's much more important to draft from the head than the tail. I love old hounds because, by jove, they finish the hunt off for you, long as some ass doesn't ride over them. Don't worry about drafting from the back, but you've got to mind the ones that are cutting the throats of your good honest hounds because if you have one for three weeks doing that, you'll have half a dozen of them.

*Mr Hardaway:* You know, Betsy Park brought a bitch down and the bitch was outstanding. She could fly. None of my hounds could stay with her and I said, 'well now, we got two choices. We can try to breed a pack that could stay with her or we can give her away.' But, I said, 'you'll never breed a pack to stay with her because she don't mean for any pack to stay with her.'

*Captain Wallace:* They just go quiet don't they, just long enough.

*Mr Hardaway:* I think they do something. It's hard for me to tell just what they're doing but they don't have any intentions for that pack to run with them. She was just flying and she never seemed to put her head down, she was just flying. She may've been a super hound, you know, a superior hound, but she was no good to us.

*Mr Wood:* A question. Captain Wallace hunts a bitch pack and his kennel huntsman hunts the dog pack. Ben hunts a mixed pack. Would you two gentlemen elaborate somewhat on what you feel the advantages or disadvantages are of hunting only bitches versus only dogs versus the combination of the two?

*Captain Wallace:* I think a lot of the smaller countries in England hunt a mixed pack because they need to. That's the only way they can work it two days a week, but I think it's a question of what suits your temperament. I loved hunting dog hounds or a mixed pack, but the big days when we had 200 people or more out, I used to take the bitches if I could. They just were that little bit quicker. I think for some people, with a bit more patience, dog hounds suit them better. The late Duke of Beaufort always hunted, or nearly always hunted, bitches only. I think he hunted two packs of bitches when he was young and most of his life he just hunted two days a week and a pack of bitches, by jove, they were good as well, but his father always hunted dog hounds. He was a big man and Master told me that his father's dog hounds would ignore fresh foxes like a lot of hounds ignore rabbits, very steady, very staunch but you couldn't pull their legs.

*Mr Hardaway:* Well, I've got enough hounds to hunt a bitch pack and a dog pack and I've tried it but, like Ronnie said, it didn't suit me. I don't know exactly why. When the bitches were running they sounded too light. It didn't sound right to me. And then when I ran the dog hounds they didn't seem to have quite the dash and quite the zip that the mixed ones have, so I just went back to hunting a mixed pack. It just sort of suited me better.

*Captain Wallace:* Very few people keep enough dog hounds to have just a straight dog pack nowadays.

*Mr Hardaway:* I keep about two thirds bitches and one third dog

83

hounds. If you added mine up, I keep a good many more bitches than I do dog hounds.

*Captain Wallace:* Some of the old Masters years ago used to geld their lighter dog hounds, and they said they were marvellously keen and single-minded fox hunters.

*Mr Wood:* That's all they had left to think about. Does anybody else have a question?

*Question:* We talked earlier about how many years of experience these two gentlemen have. I was wondering if they keep any records or diaries of everyday's hunting or . . .

*Captain Wallace:* Yes, oh yes. Do you do that?

*Mr Hardaway:* Yeah, I do and I keep it in a little notebook and then, about once a year, I sit down and transfer it to a ledger type thing and embellish on the runs (LAUGHTER) and then I add up the tally of red fox, grey fox, bobcats and now, coyote, every year. Ronnie wouldn't tell you how many, but I could go back and add up how many I've accounted for since about 1960. Wouldn't be what Ronnie accounts for in two years, but still it's a lot of fox.

*Captain Wallace:* Of course you're a younger man but . . .

*Mr Hardaway:* I'm four months younger than Ronnie. We'll get this straight right now: he was born in May, and I was born in September 1919.

*Captain Wallace:* You've got it wrong. The gap is much narrower. Mr Chairman, can I ask my friend one question?

*Mr Wood:* Please do, sir.

*Captain Wallace:* In one of the daily papers on the last Saturday, there was a marvellous article about your competition, if that's the word for it, in the Piedmont country. It was a very fine illustration of the Midland hounds going through a river or a brook or a creek or something, and the water was splashing and they were all together, and I could see they were a fine pack of hounds. But the only thing that worried me, and I must just ask the Master, is, there was a picture of him going along, but he had his mouth half open. I'm very keen to know the significance of that, because if we saw the fox just like that, we'd have him.

*Mr Hardaway:* Well, as usual, I probably was cheering them on or talking or something.

*Captain Wallace:* Very fine photograph. I know that I've got a copy of it back where I left it in the hotel.

*Question:* When you're deciding which bitches to breed, do you go strictly by the individual? Say you have a bitch that you really like and she's done well but the rest of her litter may be rangy.

Would you still breed to her based on her characteristics, or would you go by some of the characteristics of the entire litter to decide?

*Captain Wallace:* The question is, 'do you breed from a brilliant individual when some of the rest of the litter aren't so good,' is that right?

*Mr Wood:* Yes.

*Captain Wallace:* I'd rather see a good litter, and I don't think it matters too much then which one you breed. I mean, if I went to see a dog hound at somebody else's kennels, which occasionally one does, it's very interesting to see his sisters, and then see some brothers and you may think it's just as good to use one as the

Joint Master and huntsman Marty Wood III crossing a flooded creek in Florida with the Live Oak hounds.

other. It may be, but some brothers are much more prepotent than others, and have much more character than others, and those are the ones that'll throw you the best sort. I would be chary of breeding from the chance bred one. We get a lot of these huntsmen getting round the puppy shows in the summer, and they persuade each other that good old Bonzo is a marvellous fox hound. Well, he may be, but he's a chance bred one, and I wouldn't go for that. Stick to your good tail male, your good tail female, and breed from good lesson. I don't think it matters a bit. People ring me up and say; 'We're gonna breed from Tulip or Stanza' or something else. I say, how the devil do you know you are, because there's something else got to happen before you can start breeding from them? We had some bitches arrived at our place once in a Rolls-Royce. Our kennel huntsman asked, 'Has your Master rung the Captain up?' He said, 'oh, no I don't think he has.' 'Well,' our huntsman said, 'never mind, bring the bitches in and I'll find out if it's alright to use them. When did they come into season?' The fellow said; 'Oh, is that necessary?'

*Mr Hardaway:* Well, I agree I'd much rather breed from a litter that all of them were pretty good than one brilliant individual where the rest of the litter you had to draft for some bad qualities. I will sometime if that bitch is the only bitch I've got in that particular line and I'm keen to keep that line in my kennels. I would probably go ahead and breed from her and take a chance on it. But if I had other lines of that bitch line in my kennels, I wouldn't breed from her. I'd breed from another bitch.

*Question:* I'm bringing out a lot of puppies this coming season. I'm wondering, the Penn-Marydels in my old pack love to dwell on cold trail, and it's great fun, but am I going to cause any problems with these frisky puppies if I allow the old hounds to hang on a line and work it? Would it be better to work them out and keep them going or risk letting them hang around in the woods and see what happens?

*Captain Wallace:* It's a question again of balance in your pack isn't it? You see, people pride themselves on hounds with very good noses and hounds with very good voices. Well, you can have too much of either of those because you get hounds, as you said, dwelling on the line. Which doesn't go for the hooroosh of the chase. And you can have hounds that kick up so much din that the huntsman can't get into communication with them. On the other hand, you can have hounds that are pretty quiet, and a bit light of nose, but with immense drive and they'll take you out of the parish when the fox has turned short. So it's a question of balance. I have found that a hound that dwells on the line when it's young, if you can just catch it a sharp one round the ankles, it does hurry it up for the future.

*Mr Wood:* We've mentioned tail lines several different times and it might be appropriate, Ronnie and Ben, for you to explain to the group what we mean by a tail male or a tail bitch line.

*Captain Wallace:* Yes. Well, it's the top line and the bottom line in a pedigree. It's the father, the father, the father and right back to 1800 or something, and the female line the same. I have a special book that was given to me so that you keep in your mind the line. It's so easy to lose them. Ben was talking about breeding from the odd bitch to keep the line and, by jove, they can disappear, these lines, can't they?

*Mr Hardaway:* Yeah. You can lose them in a minute. I've got a bitch I'm breeding right now. She's the only one that goes back to a certain line of bitches and I've almost lost it. Marty's got some lines in his kennels that I've lost in mine so I have to go down there and get it back from Marty. That's a good thing about letting other people have your hounds . . .

*Captain Wallace:* Oh yes.

*Mr Hardaway:* So that's a wonderful thing about letting other generous people have your hounds if you get in a tight spot and lose that line. Marty and I trade tail males and tail females lines in the hounds and then we can keep this thing going because we've got a bigger reservoir of this blood.

*Mr Wood:* Ronnie any comment on that?

*Captain Wallace:* I agree with all that. But never forget, when anybody who wants part English hounds or wholly English hounds, the value of the old English blood as it's called now, the Brocklesby in particular. That's where, you see, where it all came from. It's been fashionable the last forty years or so to decry those hounds as not having enough voice or tongue or nose and things, but they showed sport to very big crowds, very hard riding crowds, when countries were very good, and people could really get about. It was a top-class operation, and if you could breed back to some of that now, it's very valuable still.

*Mr Wood:* Ronnie, last fall when I was over hunting with you, one of the fascinating things that you said to me was that you'd be just a bit careful about how much you allowed a young hound that was very good, to be used as a stallion. Could you elaborate on that just a bit?

*Captain Wallace:* I won't let the very posh ones be used a lot until they're about three seasons. It can spoil them. We do use a hound towards the end of its first season because you can get an accident. You can have a valuable dog run over. I wouldn't do it

Ben Hardaway, Master and huntsman of the Midland pack which hunts in Georgia and Alabama.

until after the hunting had finished because it can, if they get one or two bitches, give young dogs a slightly exaggerated idea of their own importance. Equally, if you're an experienced breeder, I would breed from first season bitches because you'll get the most marvellously healthy puppies then, and you're not missing those bitches as you will in their third and fourth seasons when they become very sagacious hounds. But I would only do that if you're sure of the family.

*Mr Hardaway:* That was interesting. I'm breeding younger bitches now myself and I'm trying not to breed any bitches over about six years old, partially because of my experience and partially on account of what I read about the Labrador people. They said that they get a very poor return on pups out of bitches over three years old and that their best return on pups was on the first season, first year, bitches. First time they came in season or the second time they came in season, but that was their finest pups and that made an impression on me. I've been trying some of that and I think it's good.

*Mr Wood:* Thank you. Further questions?

*Question:* On this breeding thing, do you sometimes find that a bitch's second litter is better than the first one?

*Captain Wallace:* I hardly ever breed the same cross twice. If I'm going to breed from a bitch again I personally wouldn't mate her the same because you don't get the same result the next time, do you? I think that's what you said.

*Question:* Well it just seemed to me that sometimes the bitch's second litter is better than her first one.

*Mr Wood:* You mean regardless of the dog?

*Question:* Regardless of whom she's bred to, they seemed to be bigger and stronger. I just wondered if this was your experience.

*Captain Wallace:* We had a bitch called Bangle that I had at Ludlow and at the Cotswold and I took her to the Heythrop and mated her with an old dog at the Heythrop. She only had one puppy and I thank goodness I did it because she produced a hound called Brigand, Heythrop Brigand 1954. Anybody who's interested in pedigrees, you'll find him practically everywhere now, so that was a bit of luck.

*Mr Wood:* One last question.

*Question:* I wonder if you could discuss when you start your culling or whatever the processes there are as far as the pups are concerned?

*Mr Wood:* Ben you want to take a shot at that first?

*Mr Hardaway:* I think Americans raise more pups generally than the British do on a particular bitch. I let a bitch try to raise eight pups. Then you watch them all the time and if there's some physical deformity or something you start culling. I never cull for color. You can look at my pack and tell that. I try to put them out on walk and they are raised out there. They come back into the kennels and we start entering them into the pack. You know the whole process then on up until they are entered. In the process of watching them and grading them, you know if they are too tough on deer or if they're fighters or this or that. Then they go. That's the nice thing about having enough pups every year not to have to hold on to something that you really know in your heart ought to go.

*Mr Wood:* Ronnie.

*Captain Wallace:* Yes, that is so. You want plenty of hounds. I get accused of having too many sometimes but the trouble is that if you are a smallish pack and perhaps are only hunting two days a week or something and you keep very big litters you're going to over balance your kennel aren't you? I think it's possibly better to harden one's heart and reduce the litters and breed rather more litters with the same number of puppies as a result. Before the war, these huntsmen wouldn't keep more than three, four or five whelps on a bitch and they used to get foster mothers down on the train but that's a thing of the past now. With all the modern techniques and feeding and that sort of thing you can rear enormous numbers of puppies. I mean twelve and that sort of thing. I think that if you've only got a small pack, it's probably a mistake and, rather than rear twelve on one bitch, you'd be better to rear four pups on three bitches or six on two or something like that would be my suggestion.

*Mr Wood:* We have time for one last question.

*Question:* Mr President, we also have family lines of both the Exmoor and Midland hounds. Would you be good enough to elaborate on the advantages and disadvantages of each and, of course, which is the best?

*Mr Wood:* I think the question was directed at me since I made the statement that I had the lines of both the Exmoor and the Midland fox hounds in my kennels. What did I see were the various traits would you say for strengths and weaknesses?

*Question:* Good and bad.

*Captain Wallace:* There is no bad.

*Mr Hardaway:* I wouldn't answer that.

*Mr Wood:* I ought to plead the fifth amendment because I'm sitting right here between two friends. Let me say this. When I started my pack, Ben Hardaway very, very graciously gave me a superb small draft of hounds that contained some of the very best of his old lines. We developed that pack for a long period of time using those lines, providing what we considered to be very good sport. The move to bring the Exmoor line into that was a direct result of the fabulous sport that I've seen Ronnie provide on Exmoor with those hounds. The exceptional biddability, which when coupled with the biddability of the Midland fox hounds, gave us a pack, and is in the process of giving us a pack, that literally can be stopped by one person and it does not have to be a huntsman. We do have coyotes; we do have roads; we do have areas that are closed to us and there are times when we must be able to stop our hounds. In terms of whether they're deer proof or not deer proof, I'd say they're both equal because they've been bred that way for centuries or for years anyway, since neither one of them's that old.

*Mr Hardaway:* I feel like it.

Ben Hardaway with his Midland pack, hunting in Alabama.

*Mr Wood:* They've been bred for years . . .

*Mr Hardaway:* I feel like I have been bred for years.

*Mr Wood:* To be biddable. They've been bred for years to function in potential riot situations without a problem. As far as what the cross has produced, it's produced extremely fast, very tenacious hounds that are biddable. I hunt thirty couple of hounds, twenty-five to thirty couple of hounds regularly. You rarely ever hear my whippers-in. You rarely ever see them. They're just not needed. It's an extremely biddable pack that is extremely tenacious. One thing I think the Exmoor cross has helped with and that is to make them very tenacious on the line. We have accounted for more game over the last couple of seasons since we've started introducing this cross than we ever have before. I'm very pleased with it. I couldn't say anything less sitting between these two gentlemen. But . . .

*Question:* Is the speed compatible?

*Mr Wood:* The speed is extremely compatible. One of the things that we had to do was to tighten up. In running a coyote I feel it's very, very important, that you have a level pack of hounds. I don't mean in terms of color or that type of thing but a pack of hounds that runs together so that they're not all strung out across the countryside. As Ronnie was saying earlier, yes, one or two hounds may get away but the second they come to a check the rest of them are right there with them and then they're off again, you know running as a pack. Dick Webb was with me New Year's Eve when we had the great good fortune to handle a coyote. I can say that when we jumped into the field where the hounds were running the coyote, there was fifty-three hounds there and they were pretty well between me and that door about twenty feet behind the coyote. That's the kind of thing that we've gotten with this cross.

*Captain Wallace:* Can I just say for those who study pedigrees that I'm very lucky at my time in life to have the Exmoor country, but the hounds that we're talking about as the Exmoor hounds are really the Heythrop hounds. Charles Sturman very fortunately was the huntsman before the first war, and bred some very famous dog hounds for Mr Brassey. The reason he bred those famous dog hounds was because he discovered the value of old Warwickshire before 1900, and at a time when the heavier hound had not become fashionable. Those Warwickshire dog hounds, combined with one or two female lines, principally Sir Thomas Mostyn's Lady 1801 which was from the old Bicester country.

She, poor thing, I believe bred eight litters. The Heythrop was the chief recipient of them, so that's a bit of history and the reason why our sort of hound has blended in with Ben's sort of hound which I'm sure have been bred by the night hunters down in your part of the world with equal care for perhaps as long.

*Mr Hardaway:* I think the best hound I ever got from England had at least five, and maybe six, crosses of your dog Brigand and I believe he's the best dog I ever got from over there.

*Captain Wallace:* Heythrop Chorister 1906 is the key to that.

*Mr Hardaway:* That dog was Exmoor Gainsborough 1971. Can I say something?

*Mr Wood:* Yes, please.

*Mr Hardaway:* This is a little bit off the subject, but you've read a lot about the use of radios in the hunt field and there's been a lot of controversy. In the last *Chronicle of the Horse* they named me specifically, and sort of threw the gauntlet down to me to answer the question of why it's necessary to use radios. Well, I've written a letter that I hope *The Chronicle* will publish, and I just want to

A meet of the Midland Hunt in Alabama, with Ben Hardaway hunting the hounds.

give a little bit about what the radio is all about. The primary use of the radio in fox hunting is to help protect the hound and the motorist. Any huntsman who has had thirty couple of hounds driving a red fox straight towards Route 66 in the Piedmont country or a like number of hounds close on a coyote heading for the Manchester Expressway in Georgia will appreciate the two way radio. I've been there in both cases. I've also seen sixty hounds in the middle of the Manchester Expressway with hounds being hit, motorists slamming on brakes, and almost running into each other. It's a situation you want to avoid at all costs. Think of the multi-million dollar insurance claims. The Piedmont has a truck that follows around the country. This truck has a radio and can be directed to an advantageous place to help stop hounds on the highway. At Midland, the hunt always has one whip in a truck with a radio. The truck is directed to strategic places during the progress of the hunt. This truck and whip have diverted disaster more than once. I also used the radio recently to summon the truck when my daughter broke her collar bone and had a very nasty fall. That is another comforting use of the radio that in my opinion more than justifies its use. No huntsman, professional or amateur, Jimmy Atkins and me included, need or desire to take unwarranted advantage of our quarry to show sport. Good hounds are what is needed to show good sport. I can't think of a time the radio has helped me get up on a quarry or put additional pressure on the quarry. If a fox is viewed any farther away than you can hear a holler, he would have quite a lead on you by the time you got there. I will admit the radio has kept me from being thrown out of a couple of good coyote runs. The use of the radio has been compared to the use of electronic devices to find fish. For the life of me, I can't see how the use of the radio in fox hunting can be compared to the use of electronic devices to find fish. The radio can't help you find the fox. I'm all for sticking to tradition in the hunting field as long as it does not jeopardize the safety of the hound, the horse, or the human. But time and conditions change, and if hunting is to survive, it must change. If someone could convince the travelling public to go back to the traditional horse and buggy, I would gladly give up my radios. They're a pain, they're expensive, a worry to keep working and a pain in the butt to carry. Well, I just wanted to take this opportunity to tell any of you that are using radios, there's nothing to be ashamed of. It's something that is a tremendous boon for the safety of the hunt and I think we all ought to stand up to the fact that it's not taking an unfair advantage of your quarry and it just might save a human or a horse or a hound. Thank you, I wanted to get that in.

*Mr Wood:* Thank you Ben, I agree wholeheartedly. We've run a little bit past time, and I would like to take this opportunity to thank Captain Ronnie Wallace, Chairman of the British Masters of Foxhounds Association and huntsman extraordinaire, as well as Mr Ben Hardaway the past president of your Masters of Foxhounds Association, likewise huntsman extraordinaire, for taking their time to explain some of the intricacies of the sport to which they have devoted their lives. I think we owe them a great big round of applause and thanks.

(APPLAUSE)

# CHAPTER 6

# WOODCRAFT

Hunting hounds in woodland requires special skills, especially in communicating adequately with hounds. Here, Ronnie Wallace describes venery in woodland, and advises on a huntsman's tactics on bad scenting days.

An added ingredient of good sport, the little extra that tips the balance, is experience and woodcraft in the huntsman, and to a lesser extent, the whippers-in. The basis of it all is efficient and sympathetic handling of hounds, and behind that, training – like the drill on the square for budding soldiers. Woodcraft cannot be practised without these basic skills, because it involves moving the hounds, sometimes quite a long way, to improve the day's sport. They have to do that willingly.

As in life, experience must be earned. Master started hunting the Beaufort hounds aged twenty-one. On one occasion, hounds checked and the young huntsman met his father, the old Duke, sitting watching as usual from his Ford car, terrier on his knee. The young man said that, although he had had a jolly good hunt, he did not now know where the fox had gone. To which the old Duke replied, 'Try them down that gully there.' The young huntsman returned to the pack, did as he was told, and away the hounds went. That evening at tea, he asked, 'How in the world did you know the fox had gone down the gully?' 'Always has done,' replied the old Duke.

Another Master of Hounds, still in office, told me of a very diffi-cult check where a track crossed a road. Hounds had come to the right place but the fox could have gone any of four ways. A senior Master had watched him try three of them, all without success. On his return to the crossroads, this senior Master pointed to the fourth and said: 'The fox has gone down there.' He had waited to see where the fox had *not* gone before pronouncing – a privilege born both of experience and not having to make decisions oneself.

Well-handled hounds, with confidence in their huntsman and

in themselves, will sometimes practise their own woodcraft, particularly on a difficult and windy day. Usually, huntsmen give their hounds the chance to overcome a check for themselves. However, I suggest that giving hounds a tremendous lot of time in riding country can be overdone. One must have the haroosh of the chase or sport loses its thrill.

When the huntsman does take a hand, he must cast his hounds as near as possible to the place where the last hound spoke. The shorter that cast can be made, the better – and, as a quick insurance policy, a very short turn and then a forward cast. It is often important to know where the fox has not gone, in order to discover where he has gone. If the huntsman moves to where he thinks the fox has gone and it turns out that he was wrong, then he is in rather a jam. Foxes are acutely aware of scenting conditions. In these days of motor cars and many people about in the countryside, I believe that foxes are not given enough credit for making their point. If there was ever any doubt, I have always given the fox credit for going on. It has had some rewarding results.

Woodland hunting: Ronnie Wallace (*left*) when Master and huntsman of the Cotswold (1948–52), standing next to his mentor, the distinguished hound breeder, Lt. Col. Sir Peter Farquhar who was Joint Master and huntsman of the Portman (1947–59).

If all fails through bad scent or the fox being badly headed, then is the moment for venery, which is the essence of hunting and is gained from knowledge of the countryside and the farm and wild life which inhabit it. The great Will Freeman when he was hunting the Grafton hounds, had a tremendous run and a long point on Boxing Day, a somewhat rare event. Freeman told me years later: 'It was the crows that did it.' Hounds had run nearly to Northampton, it was getting late, and they were at fault. Then Freeman had seen some crows in the distance, swooping. They were mobbing the fox.

If a huntsman casts hounds every time he sees a crow swoop he will get into difficulties. Nevertheless, on that day Freeman had almost run out of scent, the light was going and instinct told him the crows had pin-pointed his fox, and so they had. Knowledge of the countryside and the wind are all-important. During a long check, farm stock or other animals might offer clues for huntsmen to follow. In stock country in winter, for instance, cattle run a large area. If a huntsman cannot understand why the hounds will not go on, and eventually finds some steaming bullocks in the far corner of the farthest field, he will know that bullocks were the cause. Like crows, they follow a fox.

When I hunted on the Cotswolds, where there was fleeting scent and many hares, the craft involved in hunting through them and maintaining our direction could be rewarding. The good hounds – the old ones who could be trusted with hares – would sometimes stop hunting. That could mean either that the quarry was a hare (particularly late in the season when the jack hares were about) or that the fox had gone and two or three hares had gone the same way afterwards. On one occasion, with Guy Cubitt out, we had a long hunt, about a six-mile point, and got to some very bad scenting ground. The hounds flipped backwards, I turned them and they ran into a wood, put the fox up, and killed him. Colonel Cubitt said to an old boy who was out, 'Why did he do that?' The old chap said, 'Well I just signalled to him that the fox had gone on.' In fact, the fox had been a long way in front! With many hares afoot, the right thing was to nudge hounds on.

On a difficult day, if a huntsman's proper cast has failed, it might mean him 'carrying' the hounds quite a distance. This is not done by galloping along, 'pounding' the hounds, with somebody bumping them on behind, because they will not hit the line. Neither is it done by getting them into a lot of thick hedges which they have difficulty creeping through. Let them get through railings, open gates for them, that sort of thing.

Above all, it is a relief to have an intelligent person with them, perhaps a whipper-in, who will say, 'Look out! There's a hound stooping to the scent.' Great is the satisfaction to discover it – although it sometimes happens behind the huntsman's horse, which ideally it should not do.

In spring, there are days when hounds can run very fast or not at all. On a day when they cannot do much, it is a real challenge to make something happen. A great hunt can be had on such a day if the huntsman keeps the pace at full tilt. He cannot afford a conventional cast and he must trust to his skill, luck, and the indication of his hounds, and keep going. I had a nine-mile point like that once, but I would not recommend that it be done very often. When this sort of thing is necessary, good whippers-in are essential – one who sinks the wind and provides information, but yet drops out of the sky when a fresh fox intervenes, is a treasure beyond price.

Hounds which can tell the difference between a fresh fox and a hunted fox are of great value on these occasions. The first time I went out with the late Duke of Beaufort, we had a marvellous hunt seen by very few people because it was the Wednesday of Cheltenham races. Towards the end of the hunt, when the fox had run the road and a fresh fox had gone up a bank opposite, these hounds just flipped at the line, went on, hit the line of the hunted fox, and killed him within five minutes.

One of the best hunts I had in the years I was hunting the Heythrop was when we came off a bad scenting hill down into the vale. Ahead of us was grass; all looked set fair. Yet, though hounds continued to indicate the fox was on, they would not own it. As we reached the corner of Bould Wood I saw a shepherd I knew, with his dog. The shepherd did not speak, but at that moment the hounds hit the line and went on right through the wood. We had a ten-mile point. A month later I found out from the owner that his shepherd's dog had chased the fox. He hadn't liked to tell me, and I don't altogether wonder.

# Chapter 7

# Horn and Voice

R onnie Wallace was a believer in a huntsman using the minimum of horn and voice. He achieved amazing results with this technique. Rather than shout at his hounds he talked to them, and below is a description I wrote of a brilliant twenty-five minutes at the end of a day with the Heythrop when Wallace produced a hunt in the quietest manner – and ended the day by chatting to his hounds conversationally, much to their pleasure.

It was towards the end of the day, and there were not many of us left. Ronnie stood at the side of the wood and said: 'Shut up all of you. Stand absolutely still and I want to hear no hollering. Not a sound.'

With that he disappeared into a smallish, but thick, covert with his hounds. Foxes came out in all directions, but not a single hound. I was astonished; this was quite incredible.

Eventually a fox emerged, presumably heading in the direction that Ronnie wished it to go, and then came the pack; hunting as one, they swept off in a group you could have covered with a carpet, running with a great cry.

I don't remember seeing Wallace while we had a fast and brilliant twenty-five minutes round the Evenlode Vale, hounds catching and killing their fox in front of us. As they did so I saw the Master and huntsman of the Heythrop trotting through a gateway, and dismounting as he told the bitch pack that they'd been 'rather good girls'.

It was an astounding performance in the neatness with which hounds had gone away on one fox, without any noise apparent outside the covert, nor assistance from whippers-in. He probably did make his famous little toot-toot on the horn, and perhaps spoke to the hounds, but on this occasion I heard no whistle from a whipper-in waiting outside the covert. Of course the text book 'Gone Away' on the huntsman's horn is a loud, thrilling sound which enables the mounted field to be sure that hounds are now running,

100

and it is time to ride after them. Wallace could blow a marvellous 'Gone Away' when it suited him.

On this occasion, owing to the terrain, there was no danger of the field being left behind. We saw and heard hounds go away in front of us, and the Field Master had every opportunity to make sure that we could ride 'to' hounds, instead of merely 'after' them, in a really fast run across grass and fences. Hounds were always just in front of us, running sweetly over the grass, speaking to the line. I had never seen matched with such quietness from the huntsman, a swift concerted exit from covert, followed by a fast hunt. Later I asked Ronnie how he did it; how it was that all the other foxes had been ignored by hounds. Nobody else could do that. He said: 'You just wait your chance.'

Horn and voice connect huntsman with hounds, Hunt staff and with all the other people out on a hunting day, including foot and

The Heythrop hounds break up their fox with their huntsman Ronnie Wallace blowing 'the kill' during a snowy day in the winter of 1976.

car followers. The question is, How much noise should a huntsman make?

A huntsman can be either quiet or noisy as far as hounds are concerned, and as far as other people are concerned, provided he remains one or the other. In hunting, one must be consistent. It is no good making a devil of a noise on Wednesday and then going out on Thursday and, feeling a bit tired, doing everything quietly. Hounds, followers and staff will all be equally ignorant about what is going on.

Take the voice first. Like humans, hounds cannot bear to be nagged. They like to be cheered, they love being jollied along, they will put up with rebuke if they do wrong (especially when you say gently to them, 'Oh don't do that', which confidence they rather like). But if they are nagged they will take not a blind bit of notice.

Hounds must concentrate if they are to produce the right reactions. At school, one never respected an interfering instructor. If one had complicated work to sort out, it was a hindrance and a distraction if the master was constantly standing over one. Similarly, it pays for a huntsman to keep a little distant from hounds as they work out a faint line, just nudging them on rather than riding among them.

As a small boy, not really old enough to take it all in, I watched Fred Hills. He hunted hounds for Lord Henry Nevill and was beloved by those who hunted with him. A fine example of a woodland huntsman, he could blow the horn the whole length of a long ride at Eridge or Bayham. After a gap of two years along came Will Freeman who was quieter, and one had to be quite lively to stay with him. I was very impressed with the Freeman method, and when I started hunting hounds I tried to emulate that quietness in horn and voice.

A previous Master of the Cotswold, L.A. Jackson, who was very good at hunting hounds in woodlands, then said to me,'Don't get swallowed up by this silent business. Bustle them out of the woods with horn and voice.' I took some note of this advice, and what I saw of him in those Cotswold woodlands, but then I went to Gloucestershire myself, and admired the Duke of Beaufort and Sir Peter Farquhar, both of whom hunted quietly. I also often talked with Chetty Hilton-Green, one of the extra-special amateur huntsmen in fox-hunting history. There is no doubt that quietness paid a great dividend in both the Heythrop and Cotswold countries for me.

Using minimum horn and voice is the style I prefer, but what is used must be effective and informative. On Exmoor, because of the terrain, the huntsman must indiate where he is more often than in countries where proximity is greater. It is a pleasure to me now to hear how Tony Wright has adapted his methods to the Exmoor country; and when I close my eyes and listen to him cheering on the hounds, I think it is Percy Durno still.

Hounds should be spoken to in a definite manner when something definite is required of them, or when they are doing something naughty. When I was a boy one often heard, when hounds were drawing, the whip cracking, to rouse the fox. I never hear that now. What is still the case is that many whippers-in have voices like foghorns, and use them harshly in rating hounds. They should very rarely be required to rate hounds and, when they do, they should make every effort to soften the timbre of their voices. Above all, whippers-in should cheer the hounds, helping to put them together. Only when something has gone wrong is a rate or a crack of the whip permissible.

Huntsmen and whippers-in must therefore practise their voices – try it in the car as they go along (with windows closed!). A whipper-in with a high-pitched voice is admirable. Few amateur huntsmen can emulate that, but they can modulate their voices, the 10th Duke of Beaufort had a beautiful voice. I once heard a description of how he and his father were conversing across a valley, both voices perfectly tuned and intoned, and wholly intelligible.

Use of the horn, as with an instrument in an orchestra, is a great art. Provided conditions are good enough for hounds to be able to hear the huntsman, he can swing them on the horn. It is no good blowing and blowing when hounds are below the point where they can hear him, and the sound is going out above them. But when near enough to them I liked to swing them, when casting. All that is needed is just a gentle touch on the horn, and they swing. The only time when plenty of noise is useful is when you know where the fox has gone, probably when going to a holloa. I dislike hearing a whipper-in or huntsman calling, Get Away, hark! and other versions of that kind of thing.

The use of horn and voice is much affected by fashion. Many huntsmen blow Gone Away! now in the manner they were taught on a recording of David Brock's, with Stanley Barker (who had been whipper-in to Frank Freeman). Freeman used to blow a different note. George Gillson, when he hunted the

Warwickshire, had a deep horn and then he would cheer like a holloa, and it was beautiful. It was also different from what most of us do now, but provided one sticks to a method, fine.

With the Crawley and Horsham in the '30s, Colonel Guy Cubitt hunted hounds two days a week. In the Weald, where there are considerable woodlands, he learned much from Charles Denton, who could hunt a fox through woodland using horn and voice in marvellous harmony, and with great penetration. Perhaps his method was not quite so effective in the gorses and open slopes of the downs where Colonel Cubitt excelled. George Knight, my invaluable kennel-huntsman, had whipped-in both there and at the Tynedale before that, and we often discussed the requirements of the varying terrains.

It is necessary to think about the field, also. That is almost a different subject; the secret being the use of connecting files, a basis for successful Field Mastering. The Field Master, and indeed all members of the field who pay attention (some do not) must know what the huntsman intends, and they can discover this only through horn and voice. If both are used sparingly all will know, when they are used, that it is time for action. If the huntsman over-indulges in either or both, the message will be confused.

One key moment in hunting hounds is getting them away smartly when a fox has left covert. Of course, if they hunt him away themselves that is fine, but very likely there will be a holloa. Then is the time for the huntsman who has wisely kept quiet as hounds speak in covert, to make a definite noise which hounds understand. This will bring them into the open to settle on the fox's line. Only then will be the moment for him to blow Gone Away!

This can be delayed if the field is large, provided the Field Master or a connecting file is made aware that they have gone. For the field to arrive at the fox's point of departure, only to find that the hounds have not gone at all, or alternatively, that they have slipped the field, ruins the confidence between huntsman, Master and followers. Reciprocal trust between hounds and huntsman, equal trust between hunt staff and the field, not forgetting the foot-followers, makes famous sport possible.

# CHAPTER 8

# TIME AND HOW TO USE IT

K eeping up the tempo of the day is one of the hallmarks of a top-class huntsman. In contrast, a lackadaisical huntsman without the ability to infuse urgency into the sport is in danger of communicating this to his hounds with dire results.

Ronnie Wallace had the ability to 'keep the tambourine a rolling', as Jorrocks put it, throughout his long hunting career.

Even though he became a substantial figure on a horse, he crossed the country remarkably effectively, never wasting a minute, and his dexterity in drawing coverts and casting swiftly were major factors in keeping up the pace. His hounds were never in any doubt that not a second was to be wasted in the chase if they were to catch the fox.

As a follower, it was remarkable how easily you could lose Ronnie and his hounds if you did not concentrate, and if your horse was not up to the demands of a long and gruelling run.

Here, Ronnie explains some of the ways in which he achieved hunting days where time never stood still!

Time and how to use it is the essence of hunting. It governs every stage in the day. The clock ticks on in the morning. How long will it take to dress properly without an ugly rush and perhaps a spur strap breaking at a critical moment? How long to get the car to the meet and park it? How long to manoeuvre the lorry into a position where it will not block road or gateway, or force riders to mount on somebody's nicely kept grass? I am a firm opponent of hounds and horses being unboxed at the meet – people tend to ride away with their bail bandages still on – and there is no case for haste when it can be avoided, nor should there ever be.

There is the question of the time at which hounds should meet. In early season hunting, this is relevant. Like most professional Hunt staff, I much prefer mornings to evenings. One can hunt early, return home in time to keep abreast of the day's agenda, and then prepare for hunting again next morning. We had an evening meet once with the Eton Beagles, and hounds had to be stopped in the dark. I said I would never do it again. Early is always better than late.

When hunting proper begins, the meet time must suit other people in addition to huntsman and staff. Some packs, the Exmoor being one, have followers from a distance staying at local hotels; they like a proper breakfast before coming out. Farmers may have milking to do, and setting fair afterwards. To allow for all this, we meet at eleven am in the regular season. In big countries, where many people have second horses, a good rule is to advertise the meet at 10.45, and to move off at eleven o'clock. This takes account of those people who are good enough to entertain the Hunt at their houses, and allows fifteen minutes for the social side to be enjoyed by hosts and guests alike.

When I was a boy, lawn meets were quite exceptional and special occasions. Happily nowadays they are very regular. Much depends on the whereabouts of the first draw. If this is a mile or so's hack away, hounds must get going and can settle en route. Otherwise a nice little corner nearby, where there is a possibility of a fox, is very handy for easing the time-pressure, and allowing the field to sort themselves out. Of course in a moorland country hounds can be drawing a second after they move off, and everybody knows this.

There is also the question of those people who lack time-awareness and arrive late. At the Heythrop, I had the idea of going back to wartime and meeting at ten o'clock. We tried it, but it was not altogether popular. In one discussion a charming lady follower who milked her own house cows put the issue with total realism, saying, 'I don't think it matters in the slightest what time you meet, as I come when I am ready.'

If people are persistently late, some Masters become annoyed and pull rank. Messages are sent out to culprits, via the secretary, and feathers are ruffled. I do not think this makes the slightest difference either. A better way is to alter the draw, so that nobody can be sure where hounds will be. Perhaps the huntsman is lucky enough to have a surprise draw up his sleeve, so that riders arriving at twenty past eleven find the hounds in full cry and quite a long way off. That is the most effective way of sharpening up the punctuality of some ladies and gentlemen. Those who arrive late, and cut across country to meet the hounds – and probably the fox – are an abomination.

It is with the time factor in mind that a Master plans his day. Blessed is the country where the meets are still given in the local papers, where earth-stopping is widely practised – and where the draw can be altered according to circumstances. Never is time more vital than at the draw.

It is very unsatisfactory when a huntsman goes into a thick place and rushes the drawing of it. That should be done thoroughly. However, there come moments later in the day, say two o'clock or so, when not much has gone on, when the huntsman must modify his plans. It is no good, not having had a hunt, to go on poking about unlikely places when he should really go to the certain find if he is lucky enough to have one handy. This brings us to the quandary between being in 'a bad hurry' and being too slow. We used to say that a bad professional

R.E.W. wearing the green jacket as recently appointed Joint Master and huntsman of the Heythrop (1952–77).

is forever hurrying when he should be taking it steady, and a bad amateur is too slow to keep warm. The truth is that any huntsman must have a clock ticking in his head, rather like a race-rider.

This mental clock is particularly important when going into covert. When, say, hounds single out a fox from among several afoot, and the huntsman hears a holloa from a trusted voice in the direction he wants to go, he must know three things already – what sort of scenting terrain he is in, the conditions of the day, and whether he can get the hounds on to the line.

The clock ticks on, pressing him to assess instantly whether he can get hounds away in the next two minutes on the fox he would like to hunt, or if it is already too late. Much depends on whether he has seen the hunted fox, and if that fox looks like going some-where, or whether it is a better bet to wait for another to go away. Also, if a huntsman wants a fox to face open country (particularly into the wind, which can be very important when hounds are settling to the line) there is a case for giving the fox a little bit of room, and not crowding him too early.

When I was hunting the Cotswold hounds – which is a fleeting scenting country – they usually needed to be on good terms with their foxes. One Christmas I went out with the Duke of Beaufort's near Chipping Sodbury, and the fox was holloaed away by Ted Reed. In my young way I was much impressed with the time taken by the Duke to get his hounds out of a wood. Right on time, the gate was open, Ted was there, and away they went. I asked the Duke about it later, and he told me he had known precisely how good a scenting country it was there, and so he knew how long he had in hand. That is timing, perfect timing.

Then there is the matter of time at the check. Hunting is a 'hoorooshing' sport and in most countries where you can ride, followers want to keep going with pace and no delay. In these days, because it is more difficult to get about the country, hounds may already have had their chance to 'do their thing'. Then it is time for the huntsman to do his. I do not support the idea of the chap who smokes two cigarettes while hounds are at fault. However, I have been impressed with Tony Wright, our Exmoor huntsman now. He gives the hounds more time than, perhaps, I would have done when I was his age. But he does not waste time. He and they recover the line in a nice way. There is a great differ-ence between giving time and squandering it. As long as the hounds are doing something sensible, and the Hunt staff are also doing something sensible, all is well.

Most checks are imperceptible. But a huntsman is forever anticipating a difficulty. Perhaps it is resolved, perhaps it fails to materialize. Even so, only the very unwise are not constantly alert for trouble. That is why, on the whole, the best huntsmen are criticized for being austere. You cannot gallop along singing, 'It's a fine hunting day' and expect to be a great huntsman.

The distance, given in time, which the fox puts between himself and the hounds, is obviously of paramount importance. Years ago Ikey Bell demonstrated the quality of hounds' noses in the South and West Wilts country by taking them off the line (or they may have run to ground) of the fox they were hunting and, he knowing of another, putting hounds on it, twenty minutes or more behind this second pilot. By this he showed how his hounds could work out the line and hunt up to their fox. We can still do the same in some of our hill countries in the West, in Wales and in the North. If necessary, hounds can hit the line of a fox that has been gone for some time.

We had an interesting example on Exmoor recently. It was a very wild and difficult day, and we were hunting foxes that had not previously met hounds. Eventually a knowledgeable lady said she had seen a fox go a certain way, but some time before – ten minutes or so – which in those conditions was rather a long time. However these hounds, hunting downwind, soon settled. Two miles later I saw them still only trotting along. Then they got on terms and away they went again. The hunt did not succeed, but it was interesting to see how they had worked up to the fox.

In most countries nowadays, with all the modern difficulties, the aim is to get away on terms. That means probably within four or five minutes of the fox going away from the covert. But sometimes you go away 'right on his back', say out of a hedgerow or whatever. With those foxes, as long as they get to the first hedge, they will be all right. But a fox pressed too hard to start with may not give the run expected. When some distance has been put between himself and the pack, he will do his own thing. He has then no need to hurry. He knows all about time. For the hunt, however, progress is the thing.

An ideal run comes when the fox is quite a distance in front of the hounds. In the end, for a successful run, they must start closing that gap. A dashing twenty minutes is very exhilarating, a pretty quick forty minutes is very good for the hounds, and probably as much as a horse wants at high pressure until he has had a breather. A hunt of an hour to one hour and twenty minutes is also very good. Thereafter one is dealing with longer hunts of two hours and more, and their different demands.

When we had big fields out in Heythropia, I thought it ideal to have a hound hunt for the ladies and gentlemen of say one hour forty minutes or two hours in the morning, with the field master exerting his charms and his skills. In the afternoon, when many people had gone home, then (as Richard Fleming once described it) the huntsman 'throws away cap and gown', the pressure is on, and even when hounds check, they are soon gone again. That is the true thrill of the chase.

It is absolutely correct that a fox can either travel quickly, or far, but he cannot do both. He has a good turn of speed. He can really hustle. But one does not see a fox going like a lamplighter as soon as he is out of hounds' immediate orbit. If every fox, as depicted by ignorant critics, is just being pursued headlong from A to B, hounds would catch every one of them. But that is not the way of it. He takes advantage of his knowledge of the country, and of his skills over scent.

CHAPTER 9

# FOXHUNTING ORGANIZATION

It has been said that Ronnie Wallace was essentially a traditionalist who would not always engage in some of the major changes deemed necessary to see hunting survive into the twenty-first century. In fact, he had to cope throughout his Masterships with continuing change and challenge in the environment of his sport, and in the political challenges to its very existence.

For many years he felt the best policy was to keep hunting off the political agenda in public, whilst forging as many alliances as possible with leading politicians behind the scenes. In this he was remarkably successful.

When the glare of television coverage made hunting a far more publicized issue, he worked through the British Field Sports Society as vice-chairman, and later through the Countryside Alliance in using modern public relations and communications techniques to express hunting's case as strongly as possible to the wider public.

As an octogenarian he attended CA rallies and its first march in London, and made the long journey to Edinburgh from Exmoor to protest against the Scottish Parliament's ban on hunting with hounds. He recognized fully the Alliance's achievement in gaining a far more favourable view of hunting among nearly all national newspapers so that they opposed the Blair government's moves towards abolition as unnecessary on animal welfare grounds, and as an infringement of human rights.

The following observations on hunting organization were made in the early 1970s when the urban pressures on the countryside were less intense. Later he was to preside over an increasing number of amalgamations, and agreed that they were a better solution than a pack striving to hunt an eroded country lying too close to major urban areas. Despite the pressures it was remarkable that the number of registered UK Fox Hunts remained near 200 into the new century.

His insistence on the power of the Master as an employer of staff and as the main authority in the Hunt was a theme of his Chairmanship of the MFHA although financial pressures ensured that Masterships acting for Committees inevitably became far more common in the thirty years since Ronnie Wallace expressed the views in the interview below.

He never changed his view on the structure of Masterships, and their relationship with Hunt staff, but at the end of his Chairmanship he presided over some strengthening of the MFHA's disciplinary system to ensure that Masters were more accountable. He believed the future of the sport depended most of all on the quality of Masterships, and recognized that there were increasing difficulties in finding candidates with the background knowledge who could still afford to devote the time and commitment necessary to run a hunting country at its best in an increasingly difficult environment for the sport. He had played a major role in encouraging many young people to enter Masterships and to follow the main precepts he espouses in this collection of his views on his sport.

Since then there have been further major changes which Ronnie Wallace approved as President of the MFHA. Chief of these was the creation of the Independent Supervisory Authority for Hunting, intended to demonstrate to government that the hound sports could regulate themselves adequately.

Foxhunting starts the season in good heart. It faces problems; it has always faced problems. Yet many people are thoroughly enjoying the sport, and a wonderful variety of hunting is still available throughout the length and breadth of Britain, and our neighbour, Ireland.

The fast increasing costs of hunting, pressures on the countryside, and the problems of accommodating the growing numbers of those who wish to hunt, will all have to be faced in the 1970s.

But before turning to these less comfortable aspects of the Chase, it is worth reflecting on the quality of sport available nowadays.

It has been an excellent cubhunting season. It seems to be an annual event nowadays for dry weather and hard going to persist in the autumn. Last year I would say it was as difficult a cubhunting season as we have ever experienced.

This year I think hounds have run with tremendous verve and cry, and I have heard from several people that they have had similar experience with their packs.

Personally, I have been terribly pleased because I think I have had the best young entry I have ever had in my life. As a number of other people have said the same thing, I do not suppose this is a particularly exceptional experience this year.

Victor McCalmont, Master and huntsman of the Kilkenny, wrote to tell me the other day he did not ever remember a better scenting cubhunting.

It is one of foxhunting's strengths that so many people still gain so much of their pleasure from watching hounds, and taking an interest in their work.

Yet there have always been a thousand different reasons why people go hunting, and this still appertains. I am glad to say the joy of the Chase, jumping the fences, and cutting the others down, is still possible in some countries.

The prospects for the season are therefore pretty good. Wheat prices have gone to some farmers' heads, and there is going to be an awful lot of winter wheat in some countries. But this does not really matter in the long run; we have had this sort of problem before.

The important thing is that the relationship between the farmers and hunting people is, in general, excellent. Fortunately, they are so often the same people anyway!

The farmers have very much to offer us; we have something to offer them, for we are all in the same boat. Those who are interested in the countryside in the end have got to keep together. This applies to all who enjoy and use the countryside, including ramblers.

Turning to some of the problems I referred to above, there is no doubt that the growing popularity of the sport is very much to be welcomed, but it causes some headaches as well.

The difficulty is that we want as many people as possible to hunt, but it is a question of increasing numbers of followers making up formidable mounted fields.

It is much easier nowadays for people to travel longer distances to go hunting. I believe the time has come for people who go hunting on horses to be contributors to the welfare of the local countryside, and the sport in the country where they wish to hunt.

There may be people who have big estates in one part of the countryside, and want to hunt in another. In my opinion, in most cases, they must transfer or extend their interests to the area where they want to hunt.

If they are not landowners then they must put something 'in the pool' in some other way.

Apart from financial support, which is vital nowadays, such hunting people can help in so many ways: walking hound puppies for example; taking a hand in affording the Hunt a practical relationship with local shooting interests; and in assisting the Hunt's public relations generally.

There are a host of other ways in which hunting people can give time and money to assist their sport, and the countryside in which it takes place.

Finance is a particularly acute problem in running a Hunt, owing to current inflation. This may accentuate the problem of young Masters taking over packs for the first time, or it could help to solve it.

Opening meet: R.E.W., then Master and huntsman of the Ludlow, at the opening meet of the Wheatland at Bridgnorth in 1946, with the Master, Miss Frances Pitt (1929–52), with the Wheatland huntsman George Dumble.

What is wanted nowadays is a Master of Hounds who is prepared to be a 'managing director' to run a country. At the same time, such a man or woman has got to have the traditional authority of a Master. That is how hunting runs most success-fully.

The present monetary inflation, worrying as it is, has perhaps pinpointed the problem. I do not believe Hunts will any longer be able to get Masterships which have open-ended agreements concerning the finance provided by the Master.

It may be possible to appoint a Master or Joint-Masters who will put up a certain sum towards the cost of running the country, but the country will have to find the rest.

But at the same time, the Master must still be treated as the authority. It is no good putting him in as 'senior office-boy'; the Hunt just will not run like that.

Connected with this, is the important relationship between the Master and the Hunt servants. They are employed by the Master, which is a very good thing.

Sometimes there is a suggestion nowadays that the Hunt servant should really be employed by the country or the committee, because this gives him security of tenure and more general security.

I strongly disagree with this. In the long run, I do not think this is in the interests of the Hunt servant.

As in any human enterprise, the popularity of the person 'in the limelight' tends to wax and wane.

At one moment the Hunt servant may be regarded in the country as a wonderful fellow; later he has suddenly acquired a reputation for being deaf, blind or simply idiotic.

If the Master employs him, he can ride the storm; if he is employed by the Hunt things can be much more difficult. The proper relationship between the Hunt servant and Master is then lost.

No one is more interested than myself in the welfare of the Hunt servant, and I strongly recommend that the old system prevails.

Another problem which may possibly arise is in a case where a Master wishes to dispense with the services of a Hunt servant.

If there is any doubt as to who exactly is employing the man, there may be a tendency for some in the country to say: 'Oh well, if he's getting rid of old so-and-so, then we'll get rid of the Master too'.

This can far too easily be the cause of a Hunt dispute, and in my opinion, it is an extremely unhealthy situation. It can be completely avoided by the Master being the sole employer of Hunt servants.

Looking at the broad picture of hunting in Britain now, there appears to be some slowing down in the tendency towards amalgamation of neighbouring packs.

I am quite keen on certain amalgamations, but they are not by any means easy to achieve satisfactorily in all cases. Sometimes amalgamations do not make sense on sheer geographical grounds, since they may be too divided by towns and other urbanization to be workable, a situation perhaps most frequently encountered in south-east England.

Yet I still feel it is a pity that if you have a good Hunt establishment – Masters, officials and supporters – that there should not be enough ground for them to hunt on two, three or four days a week.

In some of these cases amalgamation may still be the answer, purely in the interests of sport. On the other hand, I am not in favour of 'wholesale amalgamations' in future; there have been some very successful ones in recent years, but they need good people at the top to make them work.

It has been suggested that one solution to ease hunting's economic problems is for two packs to hunt separately in different countries, but to use the same kennels and cut their running costs.

This could work well, and has done so in one case in the North.

Sending out two separate packs from one kennel on the same day poses quite a lot of organizational difficulties, especially if you are trying to cut costs by using fewer staff than you would have in two separate kennels.

Yet such a system is certainly perfectly legitimate, has the advantage of retaining two countries with their own identities, and each retaining its annual point-to-point fixture. Personally, however, I would not wish to preside over such an establishment!

Well, all the writing there ever was will not show good sport, nor catch foxes. So let's hope we are all in for another memorable season.

In 1986 I interviewed Ronnie Wallace on his views about the direction of foxhunting in general. By now he was much less sanguine, and felt there was a downward trend in hunting practice. He was increasingly concerned about problems caused to hunting by changes in farming, and the competing claims of shooting as a sport growing hugely in popularity. Ronnie was clearly more worried at this time about the political threat and stressed the need to achieve more successful lobbying and informing of MPs.

His concerns proved to be all too accurate: in the next decade the pressures on foxhunting and the other hound sports increased notably in the areas of concern.

*Question:* Do you think Hunt amalgamations are worthwhile under modern conditions – where even small areas of country require intensive work by Hunts to keep them open?
*Answer:* Amalgamations are worthwhile. There are some in the pipeline now. The difficulty is that a number of forward-thinking Hunt chairmen may agree to an amalgamation, but it only needs one or two determined landowners in their countries to say they are not going to wear it and that stops it. There are certain areas where the map of Hunt boundaries wants redrawing altogether, but this is beyond what has proved practical so far.

The Vale of Aylesbury is an example of quite a large amount of country having been restructured. You need one or two strong personalities to see that these amalgamations come off.

On the other side of the coin, we have discovered, with the escalation of costs in the last ten years, that big Hunts are expensive to run. Some of the smaller Hunts, which can look after landowning and farming interests on a local basis, have become more attractive again.

*Q:* How do you feel that organization of a hunting country can best be achieved?
*A:* Everything depends ultimately on a good Mastership. Hunt committees are realizing this, but I am not sure they have all grasped that they have got to help a chap who is probably youngish and is going to make the Mastership a full-time job – which it is in a country of any size. They have got to contribute to his expenses in a realistic way.

There is a bit of a tendency in one or two cases where they have done this to regard the Master as a 'paid servant'. That is no good at all. The Master has got to be strong and financially viable – so that he can go on for some years, and he has got to be genuinely in the position of Master.

117

*Q:* The input of time by a Master is immense and, presumably, this amounts to a major financial contribution?
*A:* Absolutely. There are huge advantages for foxhunting.

It is wonderful the way the vast majority of farmers and landowners continue to support us. Where there is an objection, it is often nothing to do with hunting itself.

The two main problems which cause anxiety are the structure of farming and the sport of shooting. There must be much cause for concern over the way that farming is going economically and the immense change to arable instead of grass.

However, there is a lot of talk about 'set-aside' land and 'wilderness payments'. Keeping headlands for the Hunt to use in crossing arable land as, you remember, we used to encourage in the Heythrop country, would nearly amount to enough land set aside to satisfy those who claim that farmers are over-producing nowadays. This is also very good for conservation, particularly of birds, which everyone is now much more concerned about in agriculture.

The increasing value of shooting is no easy problem for hunting. Its solution again depends on a vigorous Mastership, which can communicate with shooting interests and impress upon them the importance of the two sports co-operating effectively. As hunting people we have got to accept that shooting has increased in area. But the shooting people want to think very seriously about the concept that 'money takes all', about over-production of birds on given acreages, and people coming in from outside to line shooting days. I think this is very dangerous in the long run for country life.

*Q:* What about the political threat to hunting?
*A:* I am no more worried than I was five or ten years ago. We have a lot of work to do before and after the General Election and I hope this is going to be fully explained to everybody by the Campaign for Country Sports.

We have got to impress upon politicians that country sportsmen comprise a substantial minority. We are determined to defend our interests and we will, if necessary, change our votes. We don't want party politics, but if it is forced upon us, we have to have it.

The so-called great weight of opinion against hunting is quoted constantly by our opponents. In fact, most members of the general public simply do not care about the issue one way or the other, and are certainly not active on the subject. If there is a public meeting, or any kind of gathering called to oppose the sport, only a handful attend.

On the other hand, if we call a meeting in favour of hunting in a rural area we get a full house. We have got to demonstrate the true picture of support for hunting to MPs of all parties.

*Q:* How do you feel about the general standards of the practice of hunting?

*A:* I think the trend is downward, I am sorry to say. If you have continuity of Masterships involving people who are able to devote sufficient time to it, without worries over costs, you are going to get better standards.

I think the prestige of the sport depends on turnout. For example, it is a very small thing in itself, but I see more and more huntsmen going cubhunting in collars and ties with scarlet coats. I think that is a poor way of going on. Discipline is surely the basis for performance.

There are less people born and bred to hunting nowadays, although there are plenty of keen and charming sportsmen, and there are many more opportunities to learn about the sport than there were when you and I were young.

We don't want to preach to people, but I think some Hunts could do more to educate their followers. Visits to kennels, with explanations by the Masters, and Sunday seminars offer many advantages for adults as well as Pony Club members.

*Q:* How do you think hound breeding is progressing?

*A:* It is true that hounds have become much more of one sort than they used to be. I rather wish that they hadn't, although I suppose I have had a bit to do with this.

I have been very pleased with the sort of hounds which the Duke of Beaufort, Sir Peter Farquhar, and we at the Heythrop, have gone in for. They have coped marvellously with conditions as they have developed in the hunting field.

I am not going to say that if I had had the luck to hunt Sir Watkin's hounds, or the Brocklesby, one could not probably have done just as well. I thought Neil Ewart's article in *Horse & Hound* was especially true. For instance, he stated that in the past breeders were probably more concerned to try to breed a pack of foxhounds to suit the particular needs of their country *and* huntsman. I believe our sort of hounds would cope with almost any type of country, although they might break their necks in the Fells if they carried the head they did in Gloucestershire.

On the other hand, there is much to be said for breeding hounds for people who are handling them.

I remember Peter Farquhar saying years ago that our sort of hounds were very hot stuff and not everybody could quite cope with them. Being very quick, you have got to have particularly high standards in hunting them. If you get one which is a little bit too sharp, it will spoil the rest of the pack very soon. The person who misses that cannot deal with them.

*Q:* What do you think of the outcrosses being used in kennels?

*A:* They are very interesting. There are the Welsh, Fell, Harriers, possibly the French and the Americans. The old-English is virtually an outcross – and a fine one too – in most kennels now.

I have had great success with one or two outcrosses, but I don't think you want to go too far into it. Get in through a new tail male or tail female, then bring them back in again to one's own sort. What you want from a new outcross, apart from a change of blood, is perhaps a little extra performance of one sort or another, but there are so many ingredients in a foxhound which are important that I don't think it is any good breeding for just one thing.

# CHAPTER 10

# EARTH STOPPING

The charge that foxhunters are 'unfair', or even cruel, to foxes by stopping their earths during a hunting day has long been levelled at the sport by its opponents.

Since the introduction of the Badger Protection Bill the subject gained further notoriety because of the tendency of foxes to go to ground in badger earths. Even inadvertent breaches of the law on stopping badger earths temporarily can lead to prosecutions.

Sadly, the legal protection of badgers has, according to authoritative veterinary opinion, led to an imbalance of the badger population in many areas of our countryside, and some significant degradation of the species because it lacks a predator to ensure natural culling. Farming interests have had to seek government approval for culls in some grazing areas where the badger is the agent spreading tuberculosis to cattle.

Ronnie Wallace deals openly and pragmatically with the controversial subject of earth stopping in foxhunting. His views are those not only of a great foxhunter, but a countryman and naturalist with a lifetime's close experience and concern for English wildlife.

Earthstopping is not a dirty trick dreamed up by foxhunters to outwit foxes. It produces what is best in hunting. Since hounds must kill foxes, how much better that this be done in a clean, fair hunt than by a local mining party. If all foxes were merely chased into holes and then dug out, who among us would call it good sport? Without earthstopping, that is the alternative.

It is no use saying that one could just take off one's hat to the fox, say Goodnight and go home, because realities must be faced. Somebody will be tempted to return to the earth and snare or gas him next day. Foxes have a rather better chance of escape above ground than below it.

That the fox must be controlled is unarguable. Suggestions that foxes might be allowed to let rip to find their own level are palpable nonsense, their food supply being domestic stock, game stock and wildlife. And, if the local pack of hounds kills acceptable numbers of foxes, the scale on which other, less attractive methods are used will be reduced.

The duty of the local Hunt is threefold: to generate a spirit of co-ordination in the local countryside, to show sport, and to catch foxes. The second of these is worth emphasising. Although hounds must kill an acceptable number of foxes, Hunts are not glorified pest destruction societies.

Earthstopping, efficiently conducted, results in foxes exploring more country, and therefore in better sport. Many foxes, on finding the earths stopped, are off and away for several miles, before either being killed by hounds in the open, or getting to ground in a safe place outside the area in which the earths have been stopped, or being lost. If foxes know that earths are habitually stopped, they will not waste time in circling to test out the earthstopper, but get away quickly.

Now that the Badger Act is in force, Hunts have no choice but to stop earths if they are to have success. If they do not, the foxes simply pour down badger setts, which infuriates the local farmers and, because the hounds mark there, the badgers are disturbed from their winter slumbers. Again, local – or not so local – people are then tempted to set about the fox by other methods, which might also injure the health of the badgers.

Of course it is far better all round if foxes are prevented from gaining access to badger earths. The fox going into it, the hounds arriving, and spectators following, are more disturbing to badgers and draw the attention of those whose concern it is not, to there being a badger sett there at all. Although the new Act has made more work for the earthstoppers, they do it willingly; I hope the badger-watchers treat our people with the same respect.

Local countryside knowledge is key to the earthstopper's success. New earths can be discovered in the most unexpected places. Drains appear as if by magic. A skilful earthstopper will do much of his job by walking about. My great practitioner Charles Parker used to say that he never walked the same way twice, so that he found new holes in unforeseen places.

It is very difficult in the autumn to discover every one of them, particularly so in a country like ours on Exmoor, where there are large areas of bracken. Unfortunately, though an earthstopper stops twenty holes in a particular earth, if even one of them is left open he might as well not have bothered stopping any at all. The fox will find the unstopped hole in the most marvellous way.

The number of holes in hedges, banks and fields which are created by badgers rather than foxes should not be under-estimated: they dig far more than they need, and foxes will enjoy the use of them if they can, whether they are being hunted or not. Much the best method of stopping them is with loose earth, which does not need unstopping later. Sacks and bags, although allowed by law, may be inserted only after midnight on a hunting day, and must then be removed before the following midnight.

The further merit of loose earth is that it can save the earth-stopper some work in his already full timetable. By the time the hunting season starts the badger is quietening down in his cycle of existence and many of the holes in a badger sett, when once stopped with loose earth will not be reopened until after the winter. Some people, ignorant of the ways of badgers, then think that something has been done to drive the badgers away but in fact, particularly in the winter, a badger will reopen only one or two holes for access, and leave the rest untouched.

It has been said on a few occasions that earth has been packed so tight into the hole by the earthstopper that the badgers have been unable to get out; that is of course nonsense. Badgers will bore out through anything, let alone earth, which is why their setts are such masterpieces of underground engineering.

I know it to be true that stopping badger setts does not disturb the badgers. The countries I have been in – the Cotswolds and now Somerset – have always abounded in badger earths, so I have seen my share. After all, the badger population has increased considerably despite centuries of earthstopping. Many people seem not to realize, for instance, that badgers have several holiday homes. They will leave their main earth when perhaps it has become too-much lived-in, and are then to be found in a brand new place probably not far away.

Although foxes like to live with badgers, the reverse is not so. Badgers would rather not have foxes on the premises, hunted or not. Sow badgers will drive foxes away when they have cubs, and sometimes kill them. If fox cubs are found with their skulls crushed or ribs broken, a badger will invariably be the culprit.

It is permissible by law to stop earths that show no signs of use by badgers, by any reasonable means, subject to the wishes of the landowner, but I deprecate the use of oil drums, which are not attractive to the countryside, or paper bags, unless they are buried. Unstopping is necessary only of drains. They must be unstopped, otherwise foxes cannot get out, and the idea of a fox being unable to escape is abhorrent.

In the spring, it is important for earthstoppers not to interfere with breeding earths. These should either be lightly stoped, to prevent disturbance by a fox running in, or left alone. Some Hunts once prided themselves on never so much as putting a spade in the ground after 1 November. In these cases the temptation facing huntsmen to 'chop' foxes at the beginning of a hunt is very great. Although it is legitimate if there are several foxes afoot in covert to grab one or two before the main hunt starts, I hate to see a good fox 'chopped'. As I have said, we are not a pest destruction society. I would rather account for a fox at the end of a good run than 'chop' it at the beginning.

However good the earthstopping, foxes will get to ground, and must either be dug out on some occasions and shot with a humane killer, or left. At the end of the day, if there is to be a dig, the huntsman may remain there with the hounds, but generally this work is left to the terrier man, accompanied by one or two totally reliable assistants. In assessing whether or not to dig, the Master is guided by the strength of the local fox population, and by the wishes of the landowner. Digging is not a spectator-sport for the foot people; it is a necessity for controlling the fox.

Nowadays, if the Hunt can finance it, the full-time earth-stopper, who used to be feature a century ago, is a marvellous aid to good hunting. During cubhunting, the only stopping needed is in the local coverts and surrounding hedges. After the Opening Meet, earths are stopped where hounds will draw next day, and the 'put to' in quite a big area. At the Heythrop, we had more than 150 people involved in earthstopping.

The stopping and terrier work is often taken on by a local volunteer, who is of course in the position of a Hunt servant while he is working, and responsible to the Master, who in turn is responsible for the satisfactory conduct of the sport. This includes both the Master and the earthstopper being satisfied that there are no current signs of use of an earth by badgers – not always an easy task when hounds have been there for even a few minutes. All who stop earths must be appointed and registered by a recognized Hunt.

Earthstoppers need the eyes and ears of many local people – farm workers, village postmen, and others who know their way around the countryside. The Badger Act now means that each of them must be fully briefed in the nuances of the law – which sometimes takes a little gentle persuasion when a countryman has done the job quietly and efficiently without interference for most of his life.

In the whole spectrum of hunting, I rank earthstopping as of paramount importance. In a properly conducted Hunt the Master must know the opinions, the wishes and even the whims of landowners, and that applies particularly in relation to the fox. Most landowners want to see foxes killed in satisfactory numbers. Many consider the badger to be a threat; others are very protective of the badger setts.

Almost all like to have a litter or two of fox cubs on their land; they want them to be culled; they do not want them murdered in an unsporting way; and they like the hounds to find, and to have a good run. Without earthstopping, the picture would be a good deal less rosy for foxes than it is now.

# CHAPTER 11

# MASTERSHIP IN THE SUMMER

The foxhunting year starts on 1 May and during the months before the start of hunting autumn, Masterships must engage in essential organizational work to ensure a good season ahead.

Ronnie Wallace spent much of his time in the summer judging hounds at puppy shows and major hound shows all over Britain, and in the US. He was heavily engaged in political and organizational work in the MFHA, and he found time for attendance at a great many social occasions connected with hunting. For many years he spent many days in summertime hunting the otter as Master of the Hawkstone, and he much enjoyed deer stalking in Scotland, but when he appeared at the late summer exercise of his foxhounds they greeted him rapturously. Here, he gives valuable advice on the running of a Hunt by making the best use of the summer months.

Of the ingredients which make up a successful Hunt, organization underpins all else. As next season's new Masters of Foxhounds take office, consider the structure into which they must fit. Most Hunts are organized through a committee, which generally owns the hounds, and either owns or leases the Kennels which are given over to the Master annually. Happy is the Hunt in which the Committee runs smoothly.

One of the most important appointments in a Hunt is that of the chairman who, man or woman, must be of great wisdom, infinite tact, business sense and preferably a landowning background. In my time as a Master I have always had valued backing and guidance from Hunt chairmen. The relationship is important, the committee being empowered to appoint the Mastership, with approval from the general meeting. This too can be a moment of high drama, and it is important to specify at the outset who is entitled to vote at a general meeting, and who is not. Usually vote-bearing participants consist of farmers and landowners, a subscriber element, and perhaps some puppy-walkers vote; but it must not be a free-for-all.

Those who from time to time feel hard done by should speak to a Master, and only in the last resort to a Hunt chairman. Grumbles will be aired from time to time and people who smooth things over are preferable to those who stoke-up the fire.

Approval of the general meeting having been sought and confirmed, the Mastership is, barring accidents, in place for a year from 1 May until the following 30 April. Meanwhile, if one Master resigns, the rest must offer to give up at the end of the season too. A new set-up is then negotiated, often based on past contacts. Nowadays the committee may be named as the employer of staff. I prefer the principle that they are engaged and employed by the Master. This is important for practical reasons for Masters, and for Hunt servants, because it is a promising foundation for a harmonious working relationship. Close to the centre of Hunt authority, an enthusiastic, competent Hunt secretary is a boon.

Masters may organize the country by sharing the territory, or by making one of their number responsible overall, the others taking on Field Mastership or organizing the social scene. This last is not to be sniffed at.

The position of the Hunt in affairs of the countryside is un-limited. The point-to-point, sponsored rides, hunter trials and team chases, horse shows and terrier shows, Pony Club activities, dances, dinners, parties, whist drives and darts evenings, are all serious business, hard work to their organizers and great occasions for the guests. Then there are other events in village life – council meetings and fêtes included, where hunting people participate, making up the 'golden thread' through the country-side which ties hunting into its community.

Internally, buying and handling of Hunt horses is one of the high-cost areas. A couple of lame hounds at an unlucky time is tiresome, but two lame horses can be much more serious. Hunting has no shortage of horsemen and horsewomen well able to help and advise on buying suitable horses. Keeping them sound is another matter and depends on Hunt servants riding them with discretion, not recklessly, and on stable staff with real experience.

Financial arrangements vary widely. My experience has been

with the time-honoured 'guarantee' to the Mastership. Nowadays various different systems make the committee responsible for balancing the books. The committee will in any case maintain the Kennels, provide a casualty collection vehicle for fallen stock, see to the taxes, and possibly buy the horses.

Beyond the Kennels, organization of the country is prime responsibility of the Masters. They must strike up and keep a happy relationship with all who control the land over which the hounds run. Nothing stands still. New arrivals constantly replace old friends. No matter how small the patch of land, Masters must make every effort to meet them, and repeat the process again and again. Masters rely on the country grapevine to learn of changes of circumstance. Land agents can be a great help too.

The up-to-date crop situation must be always in a Master's

Serious business: judging a puppy show. Sir Peter Farquhar and Ronnie Wallace, with Heythrop huntsman (1937–52) Percy Durno on the left.

mind. Keeping the country open plays a tremendous part in the sport – ensuring wire is taken down and posts-and-rails put up in convenient places. New bridges become necessary, holes in older bridges must be mended. Fox coverts have to be maintained, keeping them thick enough for foxes to live in, lying above ground through winter.

Engagement of earthstoppers is vital, and more difficult now that all earthstoppers and those who help with terrier work must be registered. Blessed is the Hunt which has a skilful, congenial and sensible professional terrier man. Between the wars, Hunts did not have such people. After the second war Charles Parker helped me at the Ludlow, Cotswold and Heythrop and in effect set up the present-day system.

Many human qualities are necessary for Mastership, one being an ability to fully understand the ethics of sport. A level temperament, and ability to soothe are also important as is, occasionally, the determination to stand firm. The increasing number of Joint Masters has split up hunting countries to a greater degree than before. A professional huntsman might find himself performing on Wednesdays for a Master with an outlook different from that

A highlight of the summer season: the Duke of Beaufort's puppy show at Badminton. *L. to r.* at the 1994 show Joint Masters Capt. Ian Farquhar and the Duke of Beaufort, and the puppy show judges Capt. Ronnie Wallace and Capt. Charlie Barclay.

of the Master he hunts for on Mondays. These days of dimin-
ishing leisure-time justify the need for Joint Masterships – so long
as vital tasks do not slip through the net.

Not all Masters think alike. One of my predecessors at the
Heythrop arranged the entire season's meets while on his yacht
in the Mediterranean. The best I could do when hunting four and
five days a week, and to do it fairly, was to send out a weekly
card. The tenth Duke of Beaufort did the same, inviting his Hunt
secretary Simon Brown to play billiards with him at Badminton
on Sunday, and arranging the meets as they played. The Duke
preferred to win. At the Exmoor I have been persuaded to send
out cards every fortnight because of postage costs – and no
billiards either.

All this adds up to an actual day's hunting being done to a plan
which, while practical in itself, becomes flexible as the day
develops. The ultimate aim is that those who farm the land and
subscribe to the hounds look forward to the sport, knowing that
everything possible is being done in preparation, and during the
day, to develop whatever occurs to the very best advantage.

## CHAPTER 12

# JUDGING 'ON THE FLAGS'

R onnie Wallace's achievements in winning thirty-three championships at Peterborough Royal Foxhound Show, and many at other leading shows, were striking evidence of his extraordinary gifts as a hound breeder.

The championship victories enabled his leading stallion hounds to become a major influence on the conformation and type of foxhound to be found in 'modern' foxhound kennels throughout Britain, in Ireland, and the US.

His long rivalry with other leading kennels, notably the Duke of Beaufort's, added huge interest to the major hound shows for nearly half a century.

He was widely sought as a judge of foxhounds in Britain and the United States, and helped train and advise many others in this art. An unfailing eye for correct conformation and quickness of decision were notable in his judging.

His frequent visits to Hunts throughout Britain to judge puppy shows were opportunities to meet Masters and huntsmen as well as inspecting their hounds and advising on breeding policies.

Hound shows are pleasant summer occasions which give hunting people a chance to get together and discuss their sport. If the right sort of hound goes to the top, then shows make an important contribution to hound breeding. They enable hound breeders to see the best which the foremost kennels are producing, setting a standard for the future. The foxhound is pre-eminently a working animal, but he needs the most suitable conformation to perform his work successfully in the hunting field.

The first impression you get when you see a hound in the ring is most important. This is why you never want to look at hounds on a lead. The second they come into the ring they should be freed from the lead, and this gives the judge an immediate opportunity to see whether each hound has balance, activity and general quality.

If you have a standard in your mind's eye, then you can make up your mind straight away whether it is worth going ahead to consider a hound in detail.

What you are looking for in judging a hound is the conformation most suitable for speed and stamina. In the hunting field it must be able to go the fastest, and the farthest.

The two most vital areas you will consider are the elbow, which is the key to the front department, and the strength of the loin which is the key to the back department.

No fads or fancies, such as colour or eyes, should be taken into account – except curly sterns which are considered a fault as they are so ugly and hereditary; but sterns should be permitted to curl gently; it is no good expecting them to be like pointers.

The shape of the head itself does not matter much, although of

Leading foxhunters at Peterborough Royal Foxhound Show in 1965: *from left*, Duke of Northumberland MFH, Lt. Col. Sir Peter Farquhar, R.E.W. (whose doghound Heythrop Cardinal was champion), Lt. Col. Sir Watkin Williams-Wynn MFH, and Lord Margadale MFH.

132

course a hound must have a level mouth; it must not be under-shot, or over-shot. (In the same way, you reject a horse with a parrot mouth.)

Some people like a masculine head on a dog hound, but there are some very good dog hounds with sharp features; it is a good old fashioned appearance.

Ideally the foxhound's neck should be a long one, but it is nowhere near as important as the shoulders. People talk about

R.E.W. judging with Capt. Charlie Barclay, of the Puckeridge, in Virginia.

133

'neck and shoulders' as if they were the same thing, but of course they are two different features of conformation.

You might well prefer a hound with a good shoulder and a short neck, but you would not select a winning hound with a bad shoulder and a long neck.

A good length of humerus bone is most important. The shoulder blades should not appear too wide apart over the back. You should look over the top and the sides of the hound to discern the shoulder movement. There should not be a straight line from the point of the shoulder to the tip of the toes, because with this confrontation there is not sufficient 'cushion' when the hound moves its fore-limbs.

The position of the elbow gives you the clue to the quality of the shoulder; ideally the hound's shoulder and fore-leg should move with the true swing of the pendulum.

I like to see a hound step off at the walk, because then you see the length of his stride. There should be enough play for the elbow to move freely, and ideally this movement should be parallel to the body.

If a hound's elbow is stuck out then it is bound to move rather like a 'round arm bowler', but in a young hound you can often anticipate that there will be some improvement and 'filling-in' in this respect, and you should make due allowance for this.

The worst fault is an elbow which is pinned in underneath. It probably goes with crookedness in front.

You should look to see whether the hound is crooked. Does he turn his toes out? If his elbow is wrong, then he probably moves crookedly. Super straightness of the forelimbs could be a fault because you get a tendency to knuckle over at the knee; it is better slightly back.

Moving straight is more important than the legs actually being totally straight.

The forearm wants to be a strong one, in good proportion to the size of the hound.

The knee needs to have a little bit of elasticity. As I mention above, it is preferable to be slightly back rather than over.

Pasterns should be slightly sloping, rather than straight with the knee, as this all helps to avoid jarring.

You are looking for a sensible foot with the toenails evenly worn. I have seen hounds which remain sound with very slightly spreading feet.

But there are two types one definitely does not like: the very tight feet with no room between the toes for chafing; or puddingy, fleshy feet which are difficult in that they are unlikely to wear well.

A 'let down' toe is a fault, for it is a sign of foot weakness.

The foxhound's chest should not be too wide; the bosomy hound is certainly not required. Width bears so much on the movement of the hound. The chest should be sensibly in proportion to the size of the hound, definitely avoiding the other extreme where both legs are 'coming out of one hole'.

The stamina of the hound is much affected by conformation in this area. So you are looking for plenty of heart room. It is better for the rib bones to be deep rather than round, because the round bodied rib cage pushes the elbow out.

As far as the underline of the body is concerned, I do not mind a hound 'running up' a bit, but of course it should not be too narrow gutted.

It is very nice to see a back bone set in two cushions of muscle

Maintaining the standard: the Exmoor's winning two couple of bitches at the South of England Hound Show, 1984: Pocket ('82) by Scholar ('80) out of Polka (80); Durable ('82) byHackler ('78)- Kilkenny Duchess ('77), Goblet ('83) by Crawley and Horsham Bailiff ('75)-Heythrop Golden ('76) and Reason ('82) by Crawley and Horsham Bailiff ('75)-Resolute ('78).

135

so that you could roll a billiard ball down it with no difficulty.

One doesn't like these knobbly backs with the backbone sticking right out.

You can have either a straight back, or the arched loins known as 'wheel backs'. Either of these may be acceptable, but you must have the right equipment at the back to go with them.

The stern should be set on nicely, which means preferably quite high.

With the wheel back, well developed second thighs are particularly important, and the hocks should be set low and wide apart.

With a straight back the hocks may be set under the hound.

What you do not want is a hound with rather weak second thighs, hocks a long way behind, and 'cow hocked'.

There is another point worth remembering about wheel backs. They used to say that if a hound had a dip behind his shoulder then it must be a bad shoulder. This would be so in the case of a hound with a straight back, but a wheel backed hound is bound to have a slight dip behind the shoulder.

Concentration is vital in hound judging. Retain the standard in your mind's eye, and quickly discard the hounds which don't come near it.

There are probably many hounds to be judged during the day. So don't waste time – get for-orrard!

# FOXHUNTERS ALL

It was a measure of Ronnie Wallace's profound interest in other people, and his remarkable capacity for making friends, that he was so often called upon to write obituaries, and to give addresses at funerals.

I have included several examples because they throw a light on the hunting lives of hunting people from widely different areas of Britain, and they indicate Ronnie's appreciation that the quality of leadership in a Hunt is crucial to its success.

## Victor McCalmont

Some sixty-one years ago, in a school of more than 1,100 boys – and readers may have a job to believe this now – it was a moot point whether Victor McCalmont or I were the smallest there. Nevertheless, he quickly showed that his courage in standing his corner, his enthusiasm and his friendliness made up for any lack of stature. At school, he was intelligent enough with the work, boxed as a featherweight, was fond of cricket and had a sharp enough temper to deter fools. He had little need to become too involved with the beagles, as many of us were. His father had a pack of foxhounds in Ireland, his mother had another independently, and Victor had his own pack of beagles, which he started at an early age as a bobbery pack – history does not now recall whether he had a Pekinese on the establishment so early.

I recall a visit to Mount Juliet shortly after the war, when he was still away serving, and a first sight of that commanding mansion, the River Nore flowing below, the woodlands opposite, a large staff at the Kilkenny Kennels performing in sharp order under the command of David McMinn, with the stud with the Tetrarch box dominating it all; my companion remarked, 'Heaven must be like this.'

This was the scene of Victor's growing years and worthily he took up the duties and responsibilities which made it all so delightful, first under his father's and mother's aegis. Subsequently, as the leader himself, he was a generous and understanding employer of a vast labour force, a distinguished Master and huntsman of the Kilkenny, breeder and owner of many successful racehorses and administrator, as his father was, of the racing industry.

Before all this could fully develop – and he rode a winner at Punchestown in pre-war years – there was his Sandhurst training and the six years of war to experience. In this he served with honour in the Royal Dragoons and made many enduring friendships. In his nineteenth year, about the time he went to the Royal Military College, he lost his mother to whom he was devoted, and it was not until the end of the war, when he met Bunny Sutton in London, that this void was properly filled.

Bunny was bred for the life. Her father Squeak was commanding the 11th Hussars when the order came to mechanize the regiment; the Colonel considered the best way to restore morale was to resign and take the South Dorset Hounds so as to be handy for the new training areas at Bovington and Lulworth. After the war his grey bowler hat was a familiar sight with the Beaufort, or beside the river bank in pursuit of the otter, while Eileen was responsible for the Duke's – Master's – cup of tea as soon as he pulled up. A memorable pair.

Victor continued to ride both in point-to-points and under Rules, as he had in Denmark and Germany; when he resigned from the Army, he and Bunny set up house at Rathvinden and inaugurated a regime which became widely famous, even more so when they moved to Mount Juliet, a year after his father's death in 1968. What times were those that followed: three times Senior Steward of the Turf Club, to which he was elected in 1951, owner of the Stud, Chairman of the Irish branch of the European Breeders Fund, of Curragh Bloodstock, of Gowran Park racecourse, all beneficiaries of his example. He was proud to be elected to the English Jockey Club in his own right. He was a good shot and a skilled fisherman on the Nore, in Galway and in Iceland.

Master of one of the most renowned packs in the Stud Book, which his father took over from Ikey Bell, Victor showed truly great sport to local people, farmers, and his many friends. He achieved the almost impossible task of running two countries – the Wexford as well as the Kilkenny for ten seasons – and won the championship at Peterborough as well as innumerable awards at Clonmel and more recent venues. As with one or two other Masters, there could be an awkward silence if the decision of the judges at the shows or at the puppy judging was not to his liking. I do not know whether that was the case too with trainers or jockeys, or what he said when coming from Ireland to Cheltenham – Nevill Crump forgot to declare Victor's horse. All that is certain is that he was a keen winner and a good loser overall.

The background to all this was total unison with Bunny, and their incredible friendships and hospitality. In racing parlance, Bunny was a sharp competitor, and in hunting a thruster and a heavyweight one, in all senses. Victor's skill as a huntsman and lover of his hounds must sometimes have been sorely tried, by the tardiness in starting out and then by the pace his wife set to friends in the hunting field, not to mention the conviviality after hunting or racing. One man, of doubtful antecedence, sat down on the best chintz, covered in mud, and wondered aloud whether he would get his boots cleaned if he stayed on for a bit. Victor must sometimes have wondered who would appear next, but Bunny had no doubts.

Not inclined to politics, Victor was nevertheless prominent in local affairs, and was Freeman of Kilkenny city. He held strong belief in God and was a faithful attender at the church at Ennisnag, where he was buried with his ancestors a month ago.

Two great setbacks in his life were the necessity to sell Mount Juliet and Ballylinch, and, soon after, Bunny's death through a hunting fall. We saw then his true measure. He did all he could for the new owners and made a fresh life for himself at Norelands where Bunny, perhaps mercifully, had not lived. He continued to breed from his best mares and race the fillies, to shoot, and he invested in a vehicle to follow his beloved hounds, in hazardous style.

Victor took the greatest pride and interest in the lives and achievements of his children – Peter, Harry and Di – with horse and hound, besides three grandchildren. They can tell us what a thoughtful as well as fun father he was. In honouring his life with our admiration and gratitude, we can almost hear that tinkling laughter of Bunny's, ever so slightly mocking, and see his smile of welcome. As so many in various walks of life have said to him thousands of times, we say now, 'Good night, and thank you.'

## Percy Durno

Percy Durno was one of an exclusive company of truly celebrated individuals in the annals of Hunt service. His fame as an expert in field and kennel, and as a walking advertisement for all that is best in our rural affairs, has been widely recognized.

In the Yeomanry during the war, there were several officers who knew the Heythrop country well, including Lord Ashton of Hyde, and many were the tales of Percy Durno's adventures and apt turns of phrase. I do not know whether I like best the one of him presenting his horse at the Evenlode when he was merely casting his hounds – a leap not to be lightly undertaken when they are running their hardest – and saying to his horse, 'Come on, Sally, you know I hate water.' Or when, after a prolonged period of silence on a cubhunting morning, hounds fresh found – an exhilarating moment for the huntsman – he stopped by Lady Ashton, who had distinguished visitors with her, to remark, 'My pullets have started laying.'

Born on Midsummer's Day 1903 to a gamekeeper's family in Lincolnshire, his first post in livery was with Sir Charles Wiggin at Brocklesby. Sir Charles told me that after the opening meet, a smart occasion, and the first hunt, the new second whipper-in eventually appeared with cap askew, muddy breeches and grass in his tail buttons. 'What on earth have you been doing?' Sir Charles had asked, to be told, 'My word (his great expression) Sir Charles, my horse tripped over a turnip.' He was never a great respector of cloth, as Lord Ashton found when his huntsman more or less went to ground in his brand new green coat, obtained of course at much trouble and expense.

Durno (as he was always known) made an impression on so many whom he encountered. I have often heard of him as whipper-in at Essex Union on the marshes just east of London with the huntsman Will Wood. Then he went to Yorkshire with another great huntsman, Charlie Littleworth, a meticulous task-master with whom he so perfected his craft that when Sir Julian Cahn required a huntsman for the Woodland Pytchley he easily secured the post. A long-suffering uncle was gamekeeper in Geddington Chase, and did all he could to help his nephew provide good sport.

The following year he gained the coveted position of huntsman to the Heythrop, on the retirement of Jack Lawrence – only the third to hold the position in the twentieth century. Lord Ashton and he were both of a mind to produce a pack which really hunted hard in the varied Heythrop terrain, as well as entertain the field.

Percy Durno and his wife Nellie, with their charming personalities, made an immediate and a deep impression on people in all walks of life. Dukes, landowners, farmers, agricultural workers, tradesmen, roadmen – whoever. He was hard only on those who were not quite straight, and such he recognized at once.

Due to his medical category, he was classed as a vermin-catcher for his war service, and was able to keep the hounds and hunting going during those wearisome years. With meagre rations from Government-issued coupons, there was a vast amount of work to be done on top of his official duties, with little help. Hunting days meant early starts – probably leading the Lady Master's horse – and the necessity to complete a hunt in the far-flung parts of the country to be home before 'blackout'.

He was of course fortunate to have Lady Ashton as acting Master. Never did he try to take it all over, and never was his unswerving loyalty better displayed than during those years. Together they preserved the priceless bloodlines of the kennels which many of us value today. They kept the good will of the country intact, and fostered continued enthusiasm for hunting. Marjorie Ashton did once remark that Percy was so occupied she did not know that he was a very good husband – but we know Mrs Durno would not agree with that.

I myself was privileged to form a firm relationship with Durno, first through George Knight – a character in the same mould – and then as a neighbouring huntsman. One day he asked Lord Ashton whether he would mind him slipping off to the Cotswold for an hour or two's hunting. 'You don't mean an hour or two; more likely a day or two,' was the reply. However, he came, and what fun he made it.

When the time arrived for a new Heythrop Mastership to be found there were, not unusually, a good many notions and theories advanced. When I was asked by Major Ted Lyon to apply with Raymond Barrow for the position, one thing I knew for certain was that the huntsman would stay with us. This surprised many, and it must have been a great sacrifice for him to become kennel-huntsman; but his devotion to his friends and admirers throughout the country, to the hounds which he had cherished for fourteen years, and to the cause of foxhunting, prevailed.

Certainly, what success I have had must owe much to that decision of Durno's in the autumn of 1951. Very soon he was able to put on his son Bruce as second whipper-in, then Sidney, son of that other famous and formidable huntsman Tom Bailey, and launched them both into long-lasting careers which continue today.

From the start, Durno was even more determined than I was that the new regime should flourish – so much so that the only difficulty was in preventing him breaking his neck when the going was hard and the vale blind. He had an agreeable temperament and phraseology which prevented any feelings being rough for long. A new member of staff's old cap was produced to get a replacement of the right size. 'Yes! A'nt it an ugly little hat,' he observed.

Great was the dismay when he announced as late as Christmas 1963 that he would retire the following May. He had worked very hard all his time, he had suffered a few falls, and he and Mrs Durno decided to stop while he was still intact. His successors have fitted in superbly, following in his mould and always with his encouragement – but he did miss it all terribly when he moved to Churchill Village that summer. Nevertheless, the solution was at hand.

Captain Evan Williams and his wife Gill were at Tipperary, and keen for his assistance. Soon Durno and his wife were regular visitors and friends at Knockayney, with Lord and Lady Daresbury at Limerick, and Victor and Bunny McCalmont at Kilkenny. In that occasionally heady atmosphere, he and Mrs Durno were never out of place and always willing accomplices – save when his lordship put him to picking up stones on a field, and when the inimitable Boodley invited him – on a young horse destined for the Heythrop – to follow her over what he later described as 'nothing but a bloomin' ravin''.

On both occasions, Durno struck. But the visits continued for twenty years, to the pleasure of all concerned. He also rode out for Dermot Daly, who was producing some nice young horses for distinguished customers, but I fancy this proved more dangerous than whipping-in.

Some in his retired position might be tempted to indicate that affairs were done better in their day. Not Durno. Ever helpful and encouraging, he was to be heard describing a visit as 'they hunted wonderful well' – although I recall his reply after going out with a real tyro, 'Well, there's plenty of room for improvement.'

He continued to be active very nearly to the end of his long life, hunting with his son at Fernie over some formidable country and, I am happy to say, on Exmoor well into his eighties. He and Nellie stood up to the difficulties of life well, notably when their eldest son, Joe, was killed in 1952, just as he was embarking on his career in Hunt service. The gap was hard to fill, but the unity which they have since enjoyed with their two remaining sons, Bruce and Raymond, and their wives and families, has been a wonder. We offer them, and particularly Mrs Durno, who was so determined to have Percy with her to the end, our loving sympathy.

## John and Kirsty Roffe-Silvester

People from many walks of life in West Somerset have been profoundly shocked and saddened by the deaths in a road accident of John and Kirsty Roffe-Silvester. They were respected and loved by so many with their devotion to each other and their friendly manner, tinged with humour. Their marriage was a delight to them both and gave so much pleasure to their families and friends.

John and his brothers had such a happy upbringing at Reaphay, which Bridget and Michael acquired when they were engaged and where, in due course, they kept the Taunton Vale Harriers as well as the Beagles and Otter Hounds. John fitted so exactly into this environment. He made his mark, with his two brothers, at his school, Downside. The Abbot and Dom Edward Crouzet, both close friends of John, took part in the requiem mass, celebrated by Provost Lynch and Don Edward gave the address at the funeral. John was a deeply religious person, a skilful gardener, lover of animals, domestic and wild, and enjoyed his parents' passion for sailing. He was interested in his farm contract and timber work as well as his vintage machinery.

Kirsty, a true daughter of a Warwickshire family, who moved to Exmoor when her father took Holy Orders to become Rector of the Exmoor parishes, shared her parents' popularity on the moor. She was educated at Leamington Spa and the Royal Agricultural College before she visited Australia for a year; she came home to a Pig Research unit, then to Staggs the Auctioneers and was currently doing invaluable work for West Country Books.

The Hounds were the main feature of their lives and that commitment to them meant that the Taunton Vale Harriers were going through a most happy period and the Roffe-Silvester Hunt, which Michael had set up thirty years ago to cover the Chipstable country, was well supported. They both had such a serene way with all concerned, particularly the farmers. At the kennels they were faithfully served by David Allibone.

They both worked for the traditions of the countryside and were such family people. Some little time ago a local man told Bridget that 'they are loved and respected in these parts,' while a Greek on a remote island described John as 'a good man, a beloved man'. John and Kirsty honoured their fathers and mothers and, above all, honoured and had deep faith in God. They leave behind a numbing sense of deep loss; but they also leave behind an infant son and daughter, Michael and Mary. May they, in due time, succeed to the values and standing of their parents; certainly both sides of the family will strive for this to happen.

The Roffe-Silvester brothers, Michael and Peter burst into the post war hunting scene at the Peterborough Hound Show of 1946 – a great occasion after the bleak years since 1939. Those two came to West Somerset with their parents from Cornwall, where they had been admirers and disciplines of Percival and Barbara Williams of Four Burrow, and indeed countrywide fame. These two were collecting a testimonial on behalf of Fred Grant's widow, whose husband had recently died while serving as the Taunton Vale Foxhounds Huntsman and they made their mark, some of it in the Bull Hotel, where many stayed for the show.

Peter assumed the position of Huntsman for Lady Portman while Michael hunted the Beacon Beagles, which they had both founded in 1940, a bold initiative which was rewarded by their skill in venery and with hounds. Following Michael's wondrous marriage to Bridget and their acquisition of Reaphay he took on the Taunton Vale Harriers and established a remarkable regime, which encompassed the Harriers, Beagles and Otter hounds, although he left the summer sport to others. Of slightly unorthodox turnout and often on an odd coloured horse, Michael's aptitude and quick eye, together with his and Bridget's happy way with people of all ranks, made him a great reputation in the west. We used to enjoy him as Foxhound ring steward at Honiton Show. The Chipstable Country, hunted by various adjoining packs, was included in this happy arrangement until Michael made a short break from the Harrier Mastership in 1966, when he agreed with the local committee to establish the Roffe-

Silvester Hunt – there was one snag. The MFHA did not usually recognize an establishment which hunted less than two days a week. However, such was Michael's and Bridget's reputation for promoting the goodwill for hunting that the committee determined to recognize this Hunt on the basis of one day a week and a privately owned pack. Michael's mastership, besides that of the Harriers for some thirty-six years, continued with his own hounds until his death in 1991 and John joined in as Huntsman and then Master too.

A somewhat different figure, he continued the pattern of enjoyable sport and friendly relationships. He was admirably calm in overcoming the more complicated developments which seem to affect countryside management in recent years. He married Kirsty Atkin and such was their devotion to the land, the garden, animals domestic and wild, vintage machinery, combined with religious conviction, that their joint stewardship of the Foxhounds and Harriers was making a profound impression in this part of England.

The hounds were of great consequence to them both. Founded on West Country Harrier bloodlines, they had a strong affinity with the Cotley and thus incorporated much of the College Valley Foxhounds strains. A friendship with Ben Hardaway, a Georgian American, introduced an American cross of the July sort while connection with the Exmoor, which provided the preponderance of the pack, included the best of Heythrop, Fell, Taunton Vale Harriers, and further American strains, as introduced by Bill Brainard, another great friend and expert on American pedigrees.

The deaths of John and Kirsty were a numbing blow as witnessed by the extraordinary attendance at their funeral; the disposal of the pack was also of concern and the readiness with which the individuals found suitable homes was another tribute to the Roffe-Silvester family, William, the nephew, succeeded to the Harriers and took with him several of the hounds and his success as Huntsman so far has been an added boon – especially at a time when we mourn the death of his father, an able Huntsman in his own right.

At a time when it is necessary to put the resources of the countryside at the back of Hunting's cause, we think gratefully of the Roffe-Silvesters' contribution and look forward to more of it in the following generations.

## Major R. E. Field-Marsham

Bob Field-Marsham was a memorable man. It is true that he had God's blessing for a wonderful and long life time, but repaid that with the infectious enthusiasm which he passed on to friends and all involved in the enterprises with which he was connected. There are some still here who can recall the family party which emerged from Ashurst Park between the wars 'the Pole' and his wife, Bob, often in fall cry, Charles somewhat quieter and Betty, solicitous and skilled at lip reading.

At Eton both boys made their way into the Cricket eleven and the Ramblers tie was ever after a prominent feature of the wardrobe. Then it was the army and for Bob the Queens Bays who were in India and there he made his reputation as a polo player of skill in a trophy winning regimental side.

Hunting was always involved and he had a bobbery pack which met often – this included Yorkshire terriers; my mother – a family friend – was present when one of these fell into a raging torrent during Dunster Polo week; he and the dog got out, although a good sportsman was drowned close by that afternoon. That was an advantage of being tall. He was among those who benefited when Guy Abergavenny engaged Will Freeman as Huntsman to the Eridge. The latter was not one to tolerate those who he called mugs, but Bob and he hit it off and when, as could sometimes happen, the first whipper-in left, he was asked to whip-in during his winter leave. One has vivid memories of that happy partnership and Freeman passed on much of his inherited skills. Actually it was better to wait for the wisdom to emerge; the answer to a question could be 'You'd like to know, wouldn't you'. One of Bob's quotations. It was a time of great sport and he took on the Foxhunting part of the Aldershot Command hounds, looked after by a character by the name of Eli Cranston and whipped-in to by brother officers. There was a black hound – Surgeon who Lord Abergavenny let him have, very fierce at an earth. They all had such fun – despite the flapping, which was occasionally Bob's habit and he made his mark there as a Huntsman in somewhat insalubrious territory. Thus it came about that the Bicester and Warden Hill took him on as Joint Master in 1936 against strong competition. This is one of the leading Midland Hunts and Clarence Johnson was the well established Huntsman; he and Bob took two days a week each and it was a cordial arrangement with mutual respect. It might not have

146

been so if they had been lesser men, as there were inevitably several stirrers in the first season. The days hunting were changed round and it all became a huge success. John and Patricia saw all that going on at first hand. Bob and G. were great friends with Peter Farquhar who was at the Whaddon next door, and Betty too, and they schemed together for the modern sort of hound, so much so that by 1939 the pack at Stratton Audley was brilliant and out paced the riders in that early good scenting winter. Tom Mair and Albert Buckle, a friend ever afterwards, were the devoted whippers-in and admirers and could recount that when they were walking out and Mr Field-Marsham approached in his car those bitches would know he was around and rush towards him, such was his affinity with them, and it was a great shame that they were getting to their best just as the war came.

Bob came home at the end, married now to Charles' widow Joan, with son Rupert, so that he was in the Nevill family too and they were such close and friendly neighbours. He emerged in 1947 as joint Master of the Eridge with John Lewes. Bob Champion was Huntsman – a great family of Hunt Servants – until he retired and the Master then took the horn. Such a happy time – Daphne Courthope, perhaps the most devoted puppy walker of all times, was several years involved, and Patricia Abergavenny, Tom Cooper as Kennel Huntsman and so many other allies. Bob had such a way with all the variety of people who play a part in the hunting country and gained the deep affection of the various personalities at Bicester and Eridge; he and Joan returned that affection. The same applied at Ashurst and he was President of the British Legion. I think I can still hear Joan at some slightly outrageous quip 'Oh Bob'.

By 1961, his back had given way, despite the ministrations of Johnnie Johnson, a penalty of being so tall; but a mark of his character was the unswerving support he gave to Brian Gupwell when he succeeded him as Huntsman. By then he was renowned as a discerning – and certainly quick judge of the Foxhound and was widely invited to Puppy Shows and Hound Shows here, in Ireland and America. To have seen him sort out the most numerous and most competitive two couple class at Peterborough I have ever seen, was a revelation of its own. Puppy shows at Top Hill continued to be notable days in the hunting calendar.

Lord Abergavenny transferred the ownership of the Eridge pack to him, a source of infinite pride and, although restricted for numbers required for only two days a week, bred a pack of high class and quality on the lines which he had started and invested in years before. He was also President of the Ardingly Hound Show. All this was crowned by Freedom winning the bitch championship at Peterborough in 1964, an event fortuitously set out in the current number of *Hounds* magazine; Bob's delighted holloa rang out even clearer in the stands than when he was close at a fox among the rhododendrons at Cobbler's Hold. He was nearly as thrilled when the West Kent, who he supported so keenly, achieved a similar feat. When the Southdown amalgamation came he was pleased, although the kennels had to be further away from his home. He had so often hunted hounds on the Downs for Arthur Dalgety in years gone by. Who can forget the Centenary Dinner at Penshurst, Master Duke of Beaufort's presence there and at the Puppy Show, Bob's speech and then a spirited rendering of 'Drink puppy drink'?

Bobbie was of course a successful farmer at Top Hill notably with the cows which he bred with great knowledge and he valued his Friesian cattle connections with Mr Gibby from Pembrokeshire which he combined with visits down there to see the Hounds, David Harrison Allen, a whipper-in to him of Aldershot days, and Auriol, life long friend. But then all his friends were life long.

His shooting skills were famous and he was a most popular and sought after guest, and the dogs he owned for the sport and as companions are renowned as well. Dipper retrieved with a soft mouth, although I have an idea that he sometimes helped with getting out the fox. Stalking too was one of his passions and he went up to Scotland until late in his life, and a few years ago he was to be seen at the race meetings at Epsom, notably the Derby.

He and Joan had a great life together and her death, tempered as it was by Rupert's and his family's achievements in Canada, dispersal of the cow herd, then the illness and death of the truly faithful Bert Day, who could drive him about the country, were heavy blows, but Bob remained as exciting to meet as ever. Towards the end conversation became a bit repetitive, but his initial welcome and laugh were still so warm. He was delighted to know that the Field-Marsham strain was to continue.

'Keep smiling' he used to write at the end of his letters. So we must do just that and laugh with him as well as work on for the young to keep the sort of environment which he had enjoyed. Thank God that we knew him.

# Appendix II

# Capt. Ronnie Wallace's Masterships:

| | |
|---|---|
| Eton College Hunt | 1936–38 |
| Christ Church Beagles | 1939–40 |
| Mr Wallace's Beagles | 1940–44 |
| Hawkstone Otterhounds | 1946–68 |
| Ludlow Foxhounds | 1944–48 |
| Teme Valley | 1947–48 |
| Cotswold | 1948–52 |
| Heythrop | 1952–77 |
| Exmoor | 1977–2002 |

# RONNIE WALLACE'S CHAMPIONSHIP WINNERS AT PETERBOROUGH ROYAL FOXHOUND SHOW

Captain Wallace's foxhound breeding won thirty-three championships at Peterborough Royal Foxhound Show, the premier UK show, during his Masterships at the Heythrop and Exmoor. The list below does not include two championships won by the Heythrop just after Captain Wallace retired as their Master on 1 May, 1977, but in both cases the hounds were bred by him: Heythrop Pixton (75) won the Peterborough doghound championship in 1977; and Heythrop Draycott (77) won the same championship in 1979.

## Heythrop Champions

| | | |
|---|---|---|
| 1955 | doghound | Harper (53) |
| 1957 | doghound | Spanker (56) |
| 1961 | doghound | Blackcock (59) |
| | bitch | Clematis (59) |
| 1962 | doghound | Falcon (60) |
| | bitch | Rocket (61) |
| 1964 | doghound | Cardinal (unentered) |
| 1965 | doghound | Brewer (63) |
| 1966 | doghound | Clincher (unentered) |
| 1967 | doghound | Craftsman (62) |
| 1968 | bitch | Lupin (67) |
| 1969 | doghound | Lurcher (67) |
| | bitch | Dowry (68) |

| 1970 | bitch | Clamour (69) |
|------|-------|--------------|
| 1974 | bitch | Desert (72) |
| 1975 | bitch | Hedgerow (71) |
| 1976 | bitch | Flattery (75) |

## Exmoor Champions

| 1980 | doghound | Fortescue (77) |
|------|----------|----------------|
| 1982 | doghound | Friar (81) |
| 1983 | bitch | Durable (82) |
| 1984 | doghound | Freestone (81) |
| 1986 | doghound | Dancer (84) |
| 1987 | bitch | Pixie (86) |
| 1988 | bitch | Singsong (85) |
| 1990 | doghound | Daresbury (87) |
|      | bitch | Ripple (89) |
| 1991 | bitch | Gladness (90) |
| 1993 | bitch | Raindrop (92) |
| 1994 | doghound | Greatwood (93) |
| 1995 | doghound | Redskin (92) |
| 2001 | doghound | Emperor (97) |

# RESULTS OF CAPT. RONNIE WALLACE'S LAST PUPPY SHOW AT THE EXMOOR – 2001

Ronnie Wallace's last puppy show was packed with Hunt supporters and visitors as usual, but it was held in late summer 2001 under difficult conditions because the foot-and-mouth epidemic meant hounds would be unable to hunt normally in the 2001–02 season.

Alastair Jackson, Director of the Masters of Foxhounds Association, and his wife Tessa, Joint Master of the Cattistock, judged the young entry at Winstichen, Simonsbath.

Everyone agreed that it was one of the finest entries Captain Wallace had bred at the Exmoor. Two and half couple were by Exmoor Emperor 97, his 2001 doghound champion at Peterborough Royal Foxhound show.

Results were:

**Doghounds**: 1, and champion, Daystar, by Heythrop Sandford 97 out of Daydream 95 (walked by Mrs Lanz); 2, Blacksmith, by Derby 99-Blossom 95, Mrs J. Smyth; 3, Rascal by Lyncombe 97-Raisin 96, Miss Copp.

**Bitches**: 1, Reisling by Lyncombe 97-Raisin 96, Mrs Scott; 2, Daylight by Heythrop Sandford 97-Daydream 95, Mrs Lanz; 3, Ringlet by Lyncombe 97-Raisin 96, Miss Copp.

# INDEX

## INDEX OF HUNTS

Taunton Vale, 5, 144
Taunton Vale Harriers,
36, 143
Tedworth, 30
Teme Valley, 6, 9, 10,
149
Tipperary, 142
Tiverton, 42
Tynedale, 104

VWH, 42, 69, 70

Warwickshire, 5, 13, 92,
104
Waterford, 30
West Kent, 148
Whaddon Chase, 30,
147
Wheatland, 114

Woodland Pytchley,
140
Wye Valley
Otterhounds, 9

York & Ainsty South, 30

Zetland, 7

## INDEX OF HOUNDS

Berkeley David (81), 39
Brocklesby Nightshade
(1859), 27

Carmarthenshire
Abraham, 35
Crawley & Horsham
Bailiff (75), 135

Duke of Beaufort's
Pickwick (82), 39

Eskdale & Ennerdale
Bendigo, 42
Eton Beagles Peaceful,
48
Exmoor:
Barber, 74
Blacksmith, 152
Dancer (84), 151
Daresbury (87) 39, 40,
151
Daylight, 152
Daystar, 152
Durable (82), 135, 151
Emperor (97), 151
Fortescue (77), 39, 151
Freestone, 15, 151
Friar (81) 15, 151
Gainsborough (71),
93
Gladness (90), 42, 151
Goblet (83),135
Greatwood (93), 151
Hackler (78), 27
Pixie (86), 27, 39, 151
Pocket (82), 135

Polka (80), 135
Raindrop (92), 151
Rascal, 152
Reason (82), 135
Redskin (92), 151
Reusling, 152
Resolute (78), 135
Ringlet, 152
Ripple (89), 151
Scholar (80), 135
Singsong (85), 151
Heythrop:
Berry (78), 27
Blackcock (59), 38
Brewer (63), 150
Brigand (54), 15, 27,
37, 38, 39, 93
Cardinal, 150
Carver (38), 37
Chaffinch, 33
Chatty (62), 33, 39, 37,
93
Chorus (00), 27
Clamour (69), 150
Clematis (59), 33
Clincher, 150
Craftsman (62), 39,
150
Crystal (59), 39
Desert (72), 38, 150
Dowry (68), 150
Falcon (60), 150
Fanciful, 33
Flattery (75), 151
Flicker (75), 39
Golden (76), 135
Grossmith (71), 27

Harper (53), 150
Heather (67), 41
Hedgerow (71), 41,
151
Lupin (67), 150
Lurcher (67), 150
Redcap (82), 39
Rocket (61), 30
Sergeant (46), 37
Spanker (56), 150

Live Oak Drummer
(89), 26
Ludlow Bangle (46), 27

Meynell & South Staffs
Growler (74),39
Midland Byron, 71

Old Dominion
Gorgeous (68), 26,
31, 42
Orange County Barber
(89), 26, 43, 74

Portman Lovelock (47)
38
Portman Wizard (55)
15, 27, 38

Sir Thomas Mostyn's
Lady (1801) 27,40

West Dulverton
Romper (65), 41